The Minister Is Leaving

A PROJECT TEST PATTERN BOOK IN PARISH DEVELOPMENT

The Minister Is Leaving

A PROJECT TEST PATTERN BOOK IN PARISH DEVELOPMENT

Celia A. Hahn

A Crossroad Book
THE SEABURY PRESS · NEW YORK

Copyright © by The Seabury Press, Inc.
Designed by Nancy Dale Muldoon
Printed in the United States

Library of Congress Cataloging in Publication Data

Hahn, Celia A.
     The minister is leaving.

     "A crossroad book."
     1. Clergy—Appointment, call, and election—Case studies. I. Project Test Pattern.   II. Title.
BV664.H34   254   74-9943
ISBN 0-8164-2099-8

For Loren Mead
> Who gave me the bricks
> For this small structure,
> And encouraged me to design the roof.

Contents

Preface

CHANGE in the church—as in every other segment of contemporary society—is both constant and inevitable. Some welcome it, some resign themselves to it, others resist it; but all face it one way or another. Yet too large a dose of change all at once may lead to a crisis—what is commonly called "future shock."

One occasion in the life of a congregation demands that change should be acknowledged simply as a *fact,* not bemoaned as a problem or bewailed as an evil—that occasion when the clergyman resigns and the search begins for his replacement. Fears arise that the change will be for the worse. Hopes emerge that the change will lead to the resolution of old problems and dissatisfactions and result in a renewal of mission and ministry.

Since 1969 Project Test Pattern has been searching for reliable tools to assist in the renewal of congregational life. Much of its quest has focused on the use of behavioral science consultants in long-term relationships with local churches. Evidence has accumulated that such relationships can be fruitful, given the right conditions. But the commitment (and frequently the cost) required by the process is high, and usually some within the congregation believe that change is neither desirable nor necessary. Some feel that *renewal,* which means change, is a dirty word.

Recognizing that every congregation will change clergy

leadership eventually and that on the average such changes occur every three to four years, it became clear that such points of change could become prime opportunities for renewal in every congregation and therefore in the church as a whole *if* effective resources could be discovered and made available. Hence, a decision was made in PTP to launch a Vacancy Consultation Project,[1] focusing on the use of behavioral science consultants by congregations during those periods when they are seeking new clergy leadership.

Some of the assumptions underlying the project were that when a congregation faces the necessity of finding a new clergyman:

—It may, if left to its own resources, be overwhelmed in the confusion of unrealistic hopes and fears and make precipitous and unwise choices of its new leadership.

—It may be unusually receptive to using outside help and be able to pay for it.

—It will welcome assistance in coping with the complex emotional and social dynamics within the congregation that influence the choice process.

—Such assistance would be readily seen as a valuable supplement to the episcopal guidance traditionally available in such situation, as well as to the rational input of computerized clergy profiles made available by the Clergy Deployment Office in New York.

In general these assumptions proved themselves to be valid as the project was carried out.

In January of 1972 PTP began developing contracts with bishops in ten dioceses.[2] These contracts stipulated that during the last half of that year:

The bishops would encourage every congregation that became vacant to use the services of a consultant, skilled in behavioral science, in the search process.

The bishops would recommend consultants of their own choosing and would agree that the consultants could submit reports of their experience to PTP, assuring that anonymity would be maintained regarding particular individuals and congregations.

PTP did not attempt to be selective in the consultants who would be used or to give them any direction about how to carry out their work, although a general assumption was made that the consultants would have had prior training and experience in the application of behavioral science within religious systems.[3] In all, the work of sixteen different consultants was reported to PTP and has become the basis of this book.

Since a number of congregations that became vacant in the ten dioceses chose not to use the services of a consultant, the number of consultations was reduced to twenty-three. In seventeen of those, after the consultation was complete and a new clergyman in residence, PTP made arrangements for independent interviewers to visit the congregations to retrieve information about the effect of the consultation, as seen by the new clergyman, congregational leaders, and members of the congregations chosen at random.

The voluminous data garnered from these several sources—in several instances adding up to more than one hundred pages per congregation—were submitted to nine readers, including bishops, consultants, and theological educators. Their generalizations have formed the basis for the learnings we have now digested from the project.

Celia Hahn read fourteen files that had been completed by September, 1973, and wrote brief case histories of each one. Although she had no direct contact with the consultants, congregations, or bishops involved, she was able to read the dynamics and report the highlights of the consultations. A bishop who read her story of a vacancy consultation in his diocese said with some surprise, "I expected to read an account

written by an outsider, but it sounds like a story told by someone who was there."

This book consists of stories of what happened in those congregations, together with Celia Hahn's perceptive reflections
on the stories. She is to be congratulated for making a very in-
tense, deep, complex research project into this useful book.
This material may be read for its learnings about parish dynamics, as a guide to a particularly challenging point in the
life of congregations, or as a fascinating story of people and
their parishes.

WILLIAM A. YON

Introduction

WHAT happens when a congregation loses its minister? What are the best ways of finding a new one? Before Project Test Pattern began systematic research into the vacancy process, answers to these questions were much more tentative and partial. PTP's Vacancy Consultation Project is an initial effort to give congregations a chance to learn from other people's experiences, find better ways of working through the vacancy process, and avoid costly mistakes and useless pain.

Pain cannot be excised from the experience of losing a pastor. People cannot be protected from the grief, anxiety, guilt, and anger they often feel when their minister leaves. But they can be helped to work with those feelings so that the pain becomes "a garden, from which good things can grow," as John Fletcher, director of Inter/Met,[1] has put it. They can also be helped to take an honest look at their congregation's special needs for leadership and to work toward finding a clergyman who can fulfill those needs.

"The minister is leaving." This statement reflects an experience almost universal for parishes, clergymen, and bishops or judicatories. The positive response to William A. Yon's preliminary report on the results of the Vacancy Consultation Project, "When Change Is Not a Dirty Word," indicates the church's need for better ways of understanding and dealing with this experience. On the basis of this response, Project Test Pattern proceeded to prepare this book and a more technical, "how-to-do-it" report of the Vacancy Consultation Project for consultants, which is being written by William A. Yon. PTP's hope is that this research project will be a beginning, that further research will be conducted in order to develop and refine methods of helping parishes work through the experience of losing a clergyman and finding a new one.

This book begins with fourteen brief case histories of congregations that went through the struggle of seeking a new minister. The concluding section comprises learnings and reflections drawn from the cases. These congregations agreed to allow the church to learn from their experiences. In order to protect the confidential nature of the information, all names and places have been fictionalized, but the people who took part in the consultations will probably recognize themselves. No single person will agree with all the interpretations I have made, since these stories are put together from the words of many people, each of whom saw each incident from a unique point of view.

It is unfortunate that the necessity for confidentiality requires that these names be fictionalized, because these people, these parishes, deserve the major share of credit for the learnings in this book resulting from the research project. The participants' willingness to share their experiences, learn from them, and experiment with new procedures made possible this serious look at an important issue for all congregations.

Behind every fictional name in this book, however, stands a flesh-and-blood person. The experiences are real. The words express real feelings. The pain and the joy, the successes and the mistakes, the tears and the laughter were really there. Those bishops really exist. The commitment to the faith and to the local church are there. I am grateful to have had a share in interpreting these stories, and, even though it is not possible to give the names of the people to whom the credit is due, I want to express my appreciation for the candor and courage of the congregations, clergymen, consultants, and bishops who were willing to share a very sensitive and revealing moment in their lives so that the whole church could learn from their experiences.

Other people should be recognized for their help. This report would not have been possible without the help of John Wyatt, bishop of Spokane, who taught me a lot about the dynamics of the vacancy period and the consultative process. Loren B. Mead, Ray Averett, William E. Swing, and Robert H. Hahn also read the manuscript and made helpful comments and suggestions. I am also grateful for the encouragement to the project given by the Rev. Roddy Reid, director of the Clergy Deployment Office of the Episcopal Church.[2] The entire research project benefited from contributions of time and energy from dozens of people and groups, but a grant from the Margaret Strong Fund Committee of the Diocese of Rochester was crucial in funding a major share of the expenses.

This report of the project was written for the general reader: for clergy—those who may come to a parish and those who may go; for calling committees and vestries; for Episcopal bishops and judicatory officials in other denominations; and for people who are interested in parishes and what makes them tick. The vacancy period provides a rare chance to see the inner dynamics of a congregation's life at a moment that reveals the community's past and present life and that determines its future course.

CELIA A. HAHN
Epiphany, 1974

The Case Histories

OF FOURTEEN CONGREGATIONS

ONE

St. John's

"We were not sure we could do anything . . . . They let us know some good people might want to come here."

ST. JOHN'S is a medium-sized church in what has recently become a lower middle-class black section of a good-sized city. St. John's rector during the 50s and early 60s had been an attractive, strong leader with a vigorous style and favoring liturgical experiment, social action, and an emphasis on lay leadership and adult education. In the mid-60s, personal and professional dilemmas caused such severe stress that he resigned, leaving behind a deeply divided, confused, hurt, and angry congregation. The next rector was not able to develop his leadership abilities in the midst of all this reaction to his predecessor, and by November, 1971, he was asked by the vestry to resign.

In January, 1972, the senior warden, Mr. Charles Abbot, explored the possibility of consultative help for St. John's with the Rev. Wesley Ogden, diocesan director of clergy training. With John Olafson, rector of the Church of the Holy Comforter, and Susan Schwartz, diocesan organization development consultant, Wes Ogden came to St. John's vestry meeting. At this meeting a lively discussion dealt with feelings about the previous two rectors and the vestry's role in calling for the last rector's resignation. Discussion then shifted to the vestry's doubts of their ability to attract a good rector, or in-

11

deed, whether they felt there was a future for the church. Everyone went through a good deal of painful soul-searching, which had the effect of "grief work." Following this meeting, the vestry rushed to accept consultative help and to set parish meeting dates of March 7-8.

In his introductory remarks on March 7, the senior warden recounted the way the bishop had spoken the previous Sunday to the feelings just described, with a plea that the parish "not be disheartened. . . . This is a parish that will move into the future; scarred maybe, but into the future we will move and live and act."

John Olafson used this diagram to clarify the process of rector selection adopted by the calling committee:

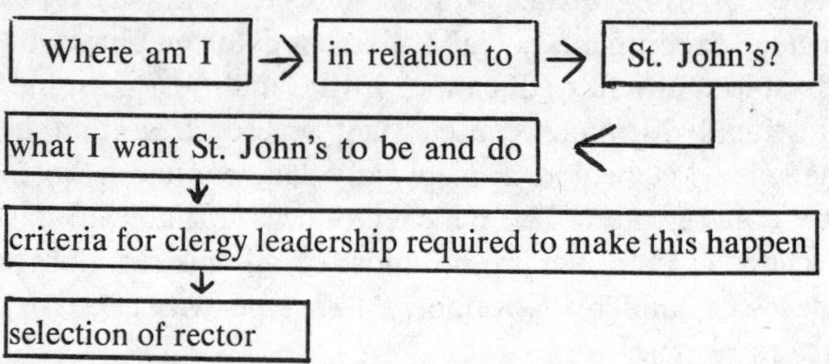

Parishioners assembled for the meeting were asked to "wield a brush," to "paint a portrait" of what they thought could be done for the parish, considering the resources on hand, by listing the things they liked and the things they felt were missing in the parish's life. The mood of the evening was spirited and open, yet the vestry's fears of being attacked on the subject of the last rector's dismissal were not realized. Ogden wondered when members would have a chance to work through their feelings about the former rectors. Olafson saw currents of disillusionment and of anger at previous clergy leadership in the lists drawn up by members.

The consultants wanted to sidestep the planned agenda to deal with these concerns at the March 8 meeting, but after consulting parish leaders they decided to follow the original plans in order to keep the momentum going. The consultants asked parishioners to study the collation of views from the previous night to identify the five most important congregational needs the calling committee needed to consider in calling a new rector. Good feelings about the meeting were evident again; parishioners spoke not only of survival but of hope and of being restored. And people seemed to be working hard to listen to different points of view in order to make diversity work at St. John's.

The calling committee developed a report carefully distilling the material from the March 8 meeting into eight areas. These areas were clerical leadership, liturgics, accommodation to diversity, education/training programs, fellowship, social outreach, lay involvement, and communications. The report was to be fed back to the congregation, shared with candidates, and used as a basis for interviewing and contracting.

The careful background paper developed by the committee analyzed the parish's recent history and described the way life with the last two rectors had resulted in extremely diversified points of view in many areas of the church's life. According to the committee, the parish's greatest need was "strong, sure, loving, spiritual leadership" of a pastor "who can convey a concern for the feelings of individuals and an acceptance of those whose values differ from his own; who can help us bridge our differences with our common faith and discover strength and enrichment from diversity."

The committee met with the bishop to share the paper and

to secure his list of candidates. (Clergy from the local diocese were to be interviewed first.) With the help of the consultants, the calling committee began training in interviewing skills, and they developed rating forms for interviewees. With the arrival of summer holidays at the end of June, Olafson reported that the consultation "sort of petered out." Possibly the committee felt overconsulted and took advantage of the summer's interruption to move away from the consultants. But the calling committee persevered in its interviewing tasks and the vacancy was filled by October 15.

On January 26-27, 1973, an interviewing team from PTP visited St. John's to gather data about the placement consultation by interviewing Stuart Heartfield, the new rector, plus the bishop and five parish groups—representatives of the calling committee, vestry, program leaders, youth and young adults, and a "cross section."

When the retrieval team asked members to look back at the departure of the previous rectors, one said, "It was rough. I still have a lot of feelings." Although parishioners reported that the consultants helped them, for the first time, to talk about the former rector's era openly, the team was aware of the grief that was still unresolved over a year after his departure.

The parishioners expressed positive feelings about the consultation, and said the consultants injected hope into the despairing congregation. "We were not sure we could do *anything*," said one parishioner, and another spoke of encouragement—"They let us know some good people might want to come here."

Comments of interviewees reflected a sense of openness and clear communication between different parties in the consultation. People seemed to be aware of the calling committee's approach and method and felt the committee had kept them well informed. They also made it clear the bishop's involvement in the initiation and progression of the consultation was important.

People seemed confident that Heartfield was just the kind of man they needed. They were very much impressed by the amount of calling he had already managed to accomplish. "He gets to *know* us," said one. "I think *people* are his priority," commented another. They agreed that pastoral care was the first priority.

The new rector said, "They felt they needed a pastor to love them, with a thick skin and a stable marriage. They needed to restore their confidence in the clergy." Provisions were made for continuing evaluation of parish priorities and the pastor's role.

On the whole, the feeling was that things were going well at St. John's, and that the placement consultation was an important reason why. One interviewee remembered that the process of finding the last rector had taken about half as long. It hadn't been a very sophisticated process, and they hadn't received much help from the diocese. This time there was a feeling of openness and good communication and participation. The senior warden summed it up by saying, "This process ought to be a pattern!"

TWO

St. Michael's

". . . like falling in love."

ST. MICHAEL'S is a historic congregation in an old Southern
town. Many of the communicants, descendants of aristocratic
families, had grandparents who worshiped in St. Michael's.
The rector, the Rev. Samuel Soules, finally resigned after
eighteen years as a moderate on racial issues—a position
that produced criticisms from both sides, only minority support from the center, and a divided parish. As one parishioner
expressed a typical response to the resignation: "Sam had been
here too long—we were glad, for him and for us." Some respondents to the PTP retrieval team said that *fear* was a part
of the congregation's reaction, both the fear of the change that
was coming *and* the fear that nothing would change.

The anxiety produced by the leadership vacuum seemed to
be indicated by an action of the senior warden. He appointed
a calling committee and announced the names of its members
at the same vestry meeting at which the rector announced his
resignation. This precipitous and unilateral action aroused the
anger of several parishioners.

Both the bishop and the departing rector recommended that
the vestry secure the services of the Rev. Beau Barker, who
had conducted placement consultations at several churches in
the diocese. He could, they said, help St. Michael's become

clear about its assets and liabilities and determine what kind of rector it needed. Barker agreed to come with a colleague to St. Michael's on May 9-10 to work with the large number of parishioners who were invited to attend the meetings. The calling committee did not communicate clearly to the parish how and why certain members were chosen to attend. Again, there were feelings later that the meetings should have been open.

During the sessions with Barker, old wounds resulting from the parish's earlier attempts to come to terms with the racial crises were reopened and re-examined. According to Barker, "They decided that they were tired of hiding and licking their wounds and that they wanted to come back to life and get moving." An examination of members' dissatisfactions with the parish provoked some feelings of concern about whether this would hurt the rector's feelings. On the whole, both consultant and members regarded the intervention as a success.

"I went down there," said Barker, "with the belief that the parish was dead and beyond salvage. I left with a surprised belief both in them and in the consultative process we had experienced. When confronted, these aristocrats showed the strength of their bloodlines. They became decisive, and they took action." One parishioner remembered, "We did it, but he led us." Another felt, "We would have gone out and fought dragons for St. Michael's."

Wishing to include a larger number of parishioners, the calling committee progressed its work by calling a congregational meeting, which was poorly attended, and then by sending out a questionnaire, to which one out of three parishioners responded. The profile that emerged of the needed leader was therefore the product, not only of the work with Barker, but of the questionnaire, which yielded specifications like "under 40" and "no beard." One young member was exasperated: "Even Jesus Christ wouldn't meet our specifications —he had a beard!" The results of the questionnaire indicated that the parish wanted "a middle-of-the-road person."

The calling committee wanted to get moving. Out of panic perhaps, many urged that they hurry and act before school started, because no rector would want to move after that. They did not check that assumption to see if it was true. The next step was to try to fit the three names of candidates supplied by the bishop into the profile that was suggested by results from the questionnaire.

Once the calling committee had met Mark Newman, one of the clergymen on the bishop's list, nobody attempted to look further. (Interestingly enough, Newman *had* a beard *and* was over 40!) "I just liked him," said one representative committee member. The **PTP** retrieval team later said that the decision-making was "not sharply rational but a warmly human process, a little like falling in love." Newman, uncertain about leaving his present parish, was attracted by the data he saw on the sheets of newsprint from the sessions with Barker. During his decision-making period, the PTP team noted that Newman had found it helpful to discuss the call with a consultant on the bishop's staff. He decided to accept the invitation to become rector of St. Michael's.

After a short time in the parish, Mark realized the need for some mutual understandings about his responsibilities. He asked the vestry to get Barker's help in negotiating a contract. Barker and his wife agreed to spend a weekend at St. Michael's, with these purposes:

1. To collect information to allow the new rector and the vestry to develop a working agreement with one another in terms of what the congregation wants, needs, and is willing to invest in.

2. To launch the new life of St. Michael's with its new cler-

gyman with some concrete strategy based on the expressed needs of the people and of the clergyman.

Barker began the first evening by asking the sixty people present to place themselves on four rating scales:

1. How included do I feel?

2. Do my hopes for this parish's future include change or not?

3. Is St. Michael's role in this town to look after the spiritual needs of its own members or to try to meet the needs of the world?

4. Is the church meeting my needs? (Am I a "Contented Connie" . . . or a "Miserable Mervin"?)

Next, Barker and his wife grouped people who had similar feelings, to enable them to communicate and support each other. The groups were asked to list the needs they hoped their involvement in the church would meet and specific activities that met, or could meet, these needs.

After the first evening, the Barkers went over the data and grouped it in four categories: Christian education/training; Christian fellowship; personal/spiritual growth and worship; community service. These categories were "simply rough handles" under which data could be grouped. On the second evening, people chose the category that interested them most and spent the evening developing strategy to meet needs in that area. The following morning, the vestry and rector studied the data, then made a priority list of things they wanted their clergyman to be doing.

The vestry at first resisted this task: "He is an honest and respectable clergyman and we can trust him to do his job!" When reassured that this was what Newman wanted, they went ahead and struggled with the priorities, and at the end, they were excited about the process, the openness, the new understanding of what their clergyman was doing. A contract had been agreed upon. While Barker had felt the contract should have been worked out before Newman's arrival, he now thought there might be an advantage in Mark's having spent a few weeks in the parish before a final agreement was reached.

Though some felt he was too mod, objecting to his calling the disciples "guys," parishioners generally seemed very pleased with their new rector. They remarked particularly about the recent successful stewardship program and Newman's ability to draw in and appeal to young people. They were aware of the contract and of plans to renegotiate it after a year, probably with Beau Barker's "painful but necessary" help. Some said, "We like Mark, but if we compared Mark's profile and our profile they wouldn't have jibed."

Many factors had been important in St. Michael's two-step consultation and search for a new clergyman—the ideas of the consultant, the influence of the bishop, the helpful support of parishioners who had leadership training, and the consultative help a member of the bishop's staff provided for Mark Newman. But one of the marks of success was the parish's sense of owning the process. As one member put it, "Beau Barker is good, but *we* did the work. I don't know if you *need* a professional. Almost anybody could have done it."

St. Paul's

"I think I can identify with their hurt . . . ."

WHENEVER members of St. Paul's wanted to say something positive about their church, they said, "You know, we're an integrated parish." This was an important achievement, but in the summer of 1972 it seemed like their only achievement. The rector, Father Juan Soledad, a Mexican by birth and upbringing, was leaving St. Paul's. A fine preacher, he had for some time not been able to function on the levels of organization or communication in the parish. Reaction to his ministry reached a peak when he decided that the church buildings should be sold.

A series of angry meetings at which the vestry made formal charges and the rector shouted them down led to a "nasty," full-scale confrontation, with the bishop present. Bishop Strong regarded the parish as "critically ill" and approved wholeheartedly of the rector's resignation. Honesty Morgan, the parish secretary, doubted whether "anything could work to cure the illnesses of this parish, short of death."

"The destructive and agonizing departure of Juan Soledad," reported diocesan staff member Bill Holloway, "was the third messy 'divorce' that the parish has experienced with its rectors." During the past six years one rector, also foreign-born, had become involved with a divorced woman, and another had left his wife. The parish split over Soledad's departure and forty percent of the members left. It was not hard to understand why St. Paul's people were despairing about their church.

These comments were recorded at the retrieval conference:

I hope it never happens again to another parish. I hope it never happens.

We've done it so many times. Three times we've had to rebuild.

I was talking to a Baptist. He said, "Oh, you go to *that* church."

The parish was anxious to find a new minister; the bishop was anxious that St. Paul's *not* find a new minister until it had had a chance to work on some of its problems. In response to the vestry's request for names of candidates, Bishop Strong answered that he would not recommend any clergyman for St. Paul's until the parish had undergone a vacancy consultation. Feeling pressure from the congregation to get a new man, and fearful that *everybody* might leave, parish leaders were angry about the delay, and some said they felt as if their "hands had been slapped."

Consultants Holloway and Steve Whittle found little enthusiasm when they met with the vestry and screening committee to identify the parish's weaknesses and strengths. Bill spelled out the assumptions that would underlie the consultants' work with St. Paul's:

1. Each congregation has unique strengths and weaknesses that must be identified as its own.

2. You can trust people to set acceptable goals for themselves and their parish.

3. Consultants are *not* present to dictate terms, but rather to assist in procedure and share observations.

Holloway reported on the evening's progress:

As the design began there was a generalized resistance to our presence and especially to the design. . . . About 10 p.m., this consultant, upon a tide of feelings, expressed quite clearly his discomfort as a response to the obvious lack of trust in the consultant's ability to be helpful to this group in exploring the strengths and weaknesses of the parish. . . . Following this honest expression of feelings by the consultant, there seemed to be very positive response resulting in greater cooperation and trust by the group. The ten o'clock hour became rather sacramental. . . .

Though resistance was still evident, as were ill feelings between the pro- and anti-Soledad parties, the committee responded positively to the evening's work. On his return from an out-of-town conference, Holloway was therefore surprised to hear that Mr. Edward V. Bane, chairman of the screening committee, had appeared in the bishop's office to demand that Bishop Strong stop the consultation and provide names of candidates for the vacancy.

Phase II of the consultation comprised an effort to broaden the work accomplished during the first evening. With fifty additional members, the committee began to move on to the questions of what they had to offer a new rector and what they needed as a parish.

Honesty Morgan later remembered that at the third session: "The most significant thing was that they had us play some children's games—getting-acquainted games. They forced people to speak to each other who had not spoken in thirty years."

This session ended with the question, "What would you like the screening committee and vestry to keep in mind as they proceed to choose a new rector, using the information you have developed from the parish evaluation meetings?"

Bypassing plans to work out a profile with the consultant, Edward Bane submitted a brief profile to the bishop three days after the meeting. Remembering this profile, Honesty said, "They didn't pay attention to the data, nor did they tell Bill or use his help. They wrote up a profile containing about four suggestions of what they wanted."

Someone had suggested that the prospective rector be native born. The bishop refused to accept the profile.

At the December 7 session, Holloway encountered deep hostility. Bane attacked the bishops and the consultant. Holloway felt it was only with reluctance that the committee agreed to continue the consultation and to share their revised profile with him. The consultant's report to PTP, written in December, indicates clearly that sparks were flying and that Bill was deeply discouraged. He wondered whether he had been "programmed for failure," whether a church that is forced into a consultation has any chance of using it productively, whether some other kind of consultation is needed by a parish as sick as St. Paul's.

The screening committee worked up a revised profile, including a consideration of the relative importance of various skill areas, and brief analyses of the community, the congregation, and its goals for the next few years. Without showing it to Holloway, the committee sent the profile directly to Bishop Strong, who, fulfilling his end of the bargain, offered the committee five names, including that of Andrew Cross, who had been doing some of the supply preaching at St. Paul's. Cross had recently lost his job with a national church organization and been divorced. He looked at Holloway's data on St. Paul's, and one of his friends in the parish remembers asking, "Andy, would you come to this church?" and Cross replying, "You might not want me."

At the retrieval conference, Cross said, "I think they felt that no one would want to come to their parish, after the three clergy 'wars' they had had. So my saying right off I was willing to come made a lot of difference." Looking back on the process that led to Andrew Cross becoming their new rector, parishioners saw it differently:

Andy met more elements on the profile.

The purpose of the profile was to bring some objectivity into the whole thing. But the selection was still made on a subjective basis. . . . Do you like the guy?

Someone was talking about the selection, and the senior warden said, "He selected himself."

Though the priorities had been unclear, and there was no contract with the new rector, parishioners seemed to feel at a deep level that this was the right "marriage" for them. Attitudes of both protectiveness and enthusiasm for the new rector were evident.

St. Paul's parishioners looked back on the consultation with guarded enthusiasm. Negative feelings about the bishop and the consultant remained. "Our history helped make us dependent," one parishioner felt. There were those who thought the vacancy period had helped to bring members face to face. Typical evaluations of the consultation were:

"I think *now* the consultation was helpful; *then* I didn't."

"The *methods* could be better, but we're pleased with the outcome."

Honesty Morgan was thoughtful, as she described the present situation to the PTP retrieval team: "There's still a lot of pain, still a lot of healing to be done."

FOUR

St. David's

> *"The rector says that the person who was most honest with him was a 91-year-old man who told him, 'Young man, you'll never see these men again—they're here tonight to get you here.' 'And,' says the rector, 'he was right.'"*

OLD people, old families, and old money ran the town of Live Oak.

When Nancy Needham and Cynthia Pond came to Live Oak to interview members of St. David's Church, they found that the parishioners with real influence were in their seventies and eighties. Young people in their twenties and thirties had no power, nor, of course, did anyone under age twenty.

"The teenagers," reported Nancy, "can't wait to get old enough to go to college and leave home and get away from Live Oak." Old families, like the Williamses, controlled the church with their financial power and also had the power to deviate from community norms without suffering the consequences.

St. David's, with a budget of $15,000, was known as "the rich church," evidently because several of the members, who made up one and a half percent of the town's population, represented old families and old money. (Because social patterns of segregation were very strong in Live Oak, half the town's residents were not considered eligible for membership in St.

David's because they are black.) With never enough people, or enough money, it had been hard for St. David's either to find ministers or to hold on to them for very long. There were so few men in the parish that all of them were automatically appointed to the vestry, with the men who chose to be active doing all the work.

In the spring of 1972, St. David's current rector left. He had come out of retirement to take the job, and his presence was felt to be temporary. Needham and Pond found mixed reactions to his departure, all the way from those who were broken-hearted to those others who were not sorry, but "most people interviewed expressed the opinion that not much changed in the parish when the former rector left and many said they were used to not having a priest."

Bishop Tower wrote the chairman of the calling committee that, according to diocesan policy, he would be sending a consultant to St. David's for two stages of work—an immediate consultation with the vestry, and a subsequent consultation with the candidate and vestry when the church was ready to call a new man. The bishop also let the chairman know the proper procedure to follow if names of clergymen were suggested to the committee, "to let me know those names immediately in order that I can check them out and let you know whether they would be acceptable in the diocese, and whether I would recommend those names. . . ."

Consultant Barney Miller arrived at St. David's on May 10 to find a very small, confused, and somewhat resistant group of members. Miller assured them he was not "the bishop's man," but was rather a person trained to be objective and helpful to churches. Even so he constantly had to answer the question why there was such an involved process when all the church wanted was for the bishop to send a priest.

Miller worked with the group using both a checklist designed to uncover their view of the responsibilities of rector and congregation and a list of the parish's weaknesses and strengths. "I felt," he wrote in his report, "their analysis of their church weakness being no real leadership was right on target. At least the leadership was not present." Not enough time had been made available for the consultation, and Miller asked them to go on working on goals and priorities in their regular vestry meetings. In spite of the limitations of this first visit, Miller felt the members had loosened up and would be open to the second phase of the consultation.

On the Fourth of July, Barney Miller came back to Live Oak to meet with a larger group of parishioners and a candidate whose name had been submitted to and approved by the bishop. Using two colors of marking pens, Miller made lists of the members' and candidate's role expectations. These lists revealed some discrepancies. He encouraged them to discuss the areas of agreement and disagreement openly. The decisive area of disagreement proved to be racial attitudes. As one young matron put it, "I am a conservative person and probably always will be—but I can't conceive of my parish priest being more conservative than I am."

Once this issue had been clarified, people began drifting out of the room; the meeting was over, for all practical purposes. Members later expressed gratitude to Miller for handling a ticklish situation in a tactful way, and helping them to "get off the hook." Miller felt that "this process headed off a very bad situation."

A third consultation was held in October with a candidate whose name had been recommended to Bishop Tower by a priest in the diocese and sent on to St. David's. Miller provided cards with various pastoral roles printed on them, priorities of people and clergymen were listed, and everyone participated with great enthusiasm in the "card game." The discussion was very open, and only two people left before the end of the session. The next day the vestry called the Rev. Wallace Green as their new rector, and waited in hope and trembling for his response. Bishop Tower announced Green's acceptance on his next pastoral visit.

When Nancy Needham and Cynthia Pond were asked by Project Test Pattern to conduct retrieval interviews at St. David's, as PTP and the diocese had agreed, they had trouble getting Mr. Green to arrange a date. At the end of a series of mutually irritating telephone calls, the rector told Nancy Needham that his congregation was "in no way interested in doing this." The interviewers reported that parishioners were indeed unwilling to talk to them and that they encountered "a lot of suspicion." Fortunately, both Nancy and Cynthia had relatives living near Live Oak and were able to "change the atmosphere from ice to warm" by swapping "do you know" information about local people and places.

Parishioners, once thawed, agreed on one thing: "We got the right man." They saw him as *available* to them, not just as "physically present" but with a "psychological *belonging*." They were happy he was reviving church suppers and picnics, though they could not agree whether or not such events were innovations at St. David's. Nancy and Cynthia finally determined that church socials had indeed been held in the past— twenty-five years ago. Members who hadn't been around that long regarded them as new ideas.

In spite of the members' enthusiasm for their new rector, the Needham/Pond team saw problems in his position. The rector believed parishioners had done a "sell job" that was not altogether candid in their eagerness to secure him for St. David's. He felt that he had not known what he was getting into. The retrieval team suggested that ways be found to inform candidates more fully about the community.

Nancy and Cynthia also saw problems for Wally Green in his youth (how can you exert leadership in Live Oak at twenty-eight?) and in the refusal of the country club, center of town social life, to admit any clergymen. On the other hand, they felt some of the new rector's unawareness of the situation might have been his own fault, a result of his concentration on his own goal of moving into this diocese rather than another.

There was a high level of confusion and disagreement about the process by which St. David's had secured its new rector. People knew that the bishop had sent Barney Miller, and they were positive about Miller's contributions:

The card game helped us to see what kind of priest we wanted.

We all filled out a form to set priorities—it worked beautifully.

We realized that it was *our* ministry as much as the priest's ministry.

Few parishioners understood just how the calling committee was appointed, or if it had any authority. And few knew who had made the decision to call Green. Some people thought the bishop had decided what kind of man St. David's needed. The 88-year-old president of the Women of the Church said, "I've seen men come and go, and I am not at all convinced that Wally Green got here through the consultation process. I think Bishop Tower knew him and knew us and that's how he got here." And Nancy agreed in her report, "she may be right."

Driving home from Live Oak, Nancy Needham and Cynthia Pond summed up their visit in a tape recording to Loren Mead:

We think that part of the resistance they exhibited is due to the fact that they have what they want now. They wanted a priest, and the way you get one in this diocese is through a vacancy consultation. Now that they have one, they have absolutely no interest in evaluating the consultative process. . . . We think the fact anybody at all attended the interviews with us was pure courtesy.

FIVE

Church of All Saints

"We have not buried Father King yet. It has been three or four years since he died."

ALL SAINTS, Barset, a primarily blue collar, lower-middle-income parish in a Midwestern city, was having trouble finding a new rector. Initially unwilling to work with a consultant, the vestry had run through several lists of names provided by the bishop. When they finally found a man they wanted, the candidate told them he wouldn't even consider the parish until it had been through a vacancy consultation.

Mr. Henry Mickle, the senior warden, called the bishop's office and secured the names of consultants Winthrop Palmer and Ruth Dellingham. The bishop's assistant described All Saints to Palmer and Dellingham as "declining in membership and money." He added, "The leadership is very dependent and there is a problem of the handling of money in the past which isn't common knowledge, even on the vestry." After talking with the senior warden, Win Palmer prepared to visit All Saints, and noted in his log: "Mr. Henry Mickle is anxious to get started, and it sounds as if he is running the show."

Win and Ruth outlined the kind of consultative help they could provide during their initial meeting with the vestry. They were puzzled by one member's repeated pleading for help with All Saints' "deep" and "crushing" problems. Not until the end of the session did vestry members tell the consultants that he had recently been released from a mental hospital, or make an effort to help deal with his comments. "Were they testing our handling of this?" wondered Ruth in her report.

During the first two sessions with the vestry, they made plans to hold an evening parish meeting and to send a survey-questionnaire to members of the congregation. The question was raised whether or not to include members of the Green Pastures Nursing and Golden Age Home, associated with the parish. The consultants reported a general agreement that the old folks should not have a say in the process. The vestry felt they were taking over the parish. One vestry member, upset because the survey he received was not what he expected, telephoned Win. Palmer commented in his report: "People get nervous and excited when there is an intervention in their system, particularly when it is in flux."

In spite of the fact that many of them had not received letters, a number of Green Pastures people were among the eighty parishioners at the March 18 parish meeting. Comments produced by small groups considering what made life satisfying or prevented life from being satisfying at All Saints often reflected the sentiments of an older group:

"We need old-time religion."

"Don't change things just for the sake of changing."

The data seemed to indicate a lack of strong lay leadership, and a wish to rely on the rector as "*the Father* of this family." There were also comments that parishioners should know more about the problems of the church and some expressions of apparent mistrust over financial affairs. The consultants summarized the two points that stood out strongly as a "communication gap" and a desire for a "daddy" to provide unity and direction. Although the consultants felt the discussion leaders' difficulty in confronting the questions had been a problem, they thought that a good deal of sharing took place and that the data produced would be helpful.

Ruth reported that during a meeting the following week to

work on the data with the vestry, one member said to Win, "Do you mean the congregation's feeling a lack of communication with the vestry?" Another member became quite defensive, pointing out that they could not tell the congregation everything. A need for "building a climate of trust" was added to a list of primary concerns derived from the data. During the sessions after the parish meeting, Win and Ruth began to work on some process issues with the group, feeling that if they could give support to the quiet ones and quiet the powerful ones, they would get more solid data for the job description. The consultants noticed that the vestry were resistant to giving progress reports to the congregation.

"I have discovered," reported Win, "a norm that I can't explain—no talking in church about the progress of the consultation. My guess is that Henry Mickle wants to restrict the information flow. It satisfies his general rule of giving the people a little bit of information at a time to keep them happy. It also keeps him in his quiet power position."

By this time, in May, the consultants' reports began to sound discouraged. They noted that the consultation was dragging and wondered whether the vacancy consultation would effect lasting changes in the vestry's norms.

Work had progressed to the point of reading the computer print-outs from the Clergy Deployment Office in New York, when the vestry sent Palmer a letter. It informed him that, while the consultants would be welcome as observers at the next meeting, the vestry felt, "We can handle things now." The consultants' feelings of helplessness and anger when they attended the June 27 meeting as unpaid observers were somewhat mitigated by the reflection that the vestry's refusal to be dependent on the consultants might be a healthy sign. In any event, three profiles were selected. Peter Stanislowsky's was the vestry's clear first choice.

The vestry and rector-elect Stanislowsky sent the consultants a request to meet with them in July for the purpose of drawing up a contract. Win and Ruth worked with the vestry to prepare for the contract-building session, which was structured around a comparison between the job description and a position paper of Stanislowsky's. The vestry emphasized the similarities between the two documents, while the new rector pointed out areas of difference. The contract, when drawn up, included an agreement to hold an annual evaluation.

When a PTP retrieval team visited All Saints, Barset, they found members happy with their hard-working new rector. "Every day he puts in a working man's day," said one. They were clear about their rector's people-to-people priorities, and some felt they had responded to them: "We have a much closer feeling and we have warmed up a little bit." Young people felt more involved and active and were aware of the rector's interest in developing lay leadership. Stanislowsky himself told the interviewers:

"I think my major work is changing the image of All Saints to a community church—from a chapel for the elderly to a representative to the community."

Retrieval interviews surfaced strong feelings about former rectors that had not been reported during the consultation. The last rector, Father Duncan Dimly, had resigned after a two-year period. Parishioners reported reactions of relief and surprise to the departure of Father Dimly. A clergyman who had spent a large proportion of his time visiting the elderly residents of Green Pastures, and who was not popular with the young people in the parish, Dimly had not made a strong positive impression at All Saints. The bishop revealed that Dimly had discovered funds missing from the Green Pastures books and had resigned in fear that he would be held responsible for the misappropriated sum.

One has the impression that the chances of Father Dimly's

achieving a successful ministry at All Saints were slim, also, because of the popularity of Father Herbert King, who had served with the parish for sixteen years prior to Dimly's arrival. Strong feelings of grief over King's death were reported by parishioners:

He was a holy man.

I was on the way out the door when I heard the news, and I sat on the steps and cried. (*Male interviewee*)

The funeral was beautiful but it was so sad. It was like a member of the family had left.

. . . and the head of the family at that.

Asked by the interviewers about the parishioners' grief and bereavement, the new rector thought there was an "unusual amount" and commented, "Barset is a very nostalgic . . . a nineteenth-century community."

Stanislowsky saw the period of Dimly's rectorship as a leadership vacuum, with parishioners acting as though those two years had never existed.

"Whenever you try to find what direction to go," the rector said, "the vestry will say, 'When Father King was here. . . .' He is the standard by which they operate." Stanislowsky saw the power of the senior warden as one result of the leadership vacuum.

The retrieval interviews point up the norm of secrecy and consequent mistrust referred to by the consultants. When asked what they knew about the work of the calling committee or the consultants, members typically replied that they had never heard of them.

Parishioners said that Stanislowsky was working hard to increase openness and communication in the parish, despite the difficulty of the task: "Father Stanislowsky has done all he can. He has all the lines open for communication. Either the people are not interested or they mumble and grumble their displeasures."

The consultation was seen as a major intervention in the "mumble-grumble" syndrome. People spoke out openly at the parish meeting and had a real share in the selection of the new rector. Some of the vestry members who had seemed most resistant to the consultants earlier had high praise for their work during the interviews:

They made us think. They were magnificent people.

It wasn't what they did; it was what they got us to do.

If it didn't work in other places, either the consultants were not as good or the parish would not accept change.

Time will test the willingness of the people at All Saints to change. The rector is uncertain: " 'We want these things to happen but we want the church to remain the same' seems to be what some are saying. . . . I don't think they know the cost of the things they want to happen here."

SIX

St. Luke's

"When he walked in we all felt this is the man the Lord has sent."

ST. LUKE'S is an inner-city parish located in a predominately (ninety percent) Puerto Rican area. The English-speaking congregation, who support St. Luke's financially, commute to the church from the suburbs. Their rector, the Rev. James B. Lord, had asked for permission to devote ever-increasing time to his extraparochial involvement in the charismatic movement.[1] Parishioners were thus not surprised when he resigned to become rector of a larger parish in which the movement was strong. There were, however, expressions of grief:

"When he left, I came completely unglued over losing my spiritual rock."

"What's gonna happen to us?"

The bishop, as well as several members, also noticed feelings of relief, "as the parish was going down hill." Many blamed the rector's frequent absences for this declining condition.

Father Lord appointed five vestry members to be a calling committee. During retrieval interviews one member voiced this opinion regarding the appointments: "Father Jim started the charismatic movement here. He believed it must continue for the survival of the parish. He felt these five would assure it." The chairman of the calling committee, who was also junior warden, and a noncharismatic, expanded the committee to include the entire vestry. Members of the committee had received the name of the Rev. William L. Dove, possibly from the rector. Bishop Hand reported that the first time they had met with him they mentioned Dove's name and he had rejected it.

The bishop had contracted with Stuart McInnes to conduct vacancy consultations in the diocese. Bishop Hand met with the wardens, and reported later:

The process of convincing them to take a good look began. The senior warden bought it. The junior warden wouldn't buy it at first. At this point there was some "arm twisting" on my part. . . . They thought I had a preconceived notion as to what their needs were and the kind of man they should get. Yes, I did have these opinions of what they needed and the kind of man they needed. . . . I urged them to use the consultant. They had no choice.

One member said during retrieval interviews that he had heard the bishop had "taken over" the vestry's responsibility and contacted the Clergy Deployment Office. The member "resented" the bishop's move; he felt it meant "the bishop . . . didn't think we had enough sense to get our own [priest]." Bishop, CDO, and consultant—all seemed to be identified as "the other side." The consultant met with the bishop after the "arm twisting" episode, and reported:

"The bishop informed me that his big issue with the parish was in ministering to the Spanish-speaking people who lived in the immediate neighborhood, as the parish currently had only a handful of these people. . . . He further said that, if they failed to face into the Puerto Rican issue, he would intervene with them."

It was in this setting of strong actions and strong feelings that Stuart McInnes began his vacancy consultations with the St. Luke's community. During the first of three sessions, he led a group of nineteen, consisting of the calling committee plus additional members, in sharing problems and dreams for their parish. He gave them a Congregational Role Expectation Instrument to use with the entire congregation the following Sunday, and suggested they begin work on a contract. McInnes reported that the junior warden had said that they didn't want a contract. He asked why and the warden replied that they didn't need it.

The discussion at the second session, with twenty-eight members present, centered around whether or not they wanted a clergyman who was involved in the charismatic movement. The people who considered themselves charismatic really wanted such a priest. The others were ambivalent.

"This was good," remembered a participant, "because this was the first time we had a good talk about the charismatic movement—differences were aired between the charismatics and the noncharismatics."

During the third session, the outreach statement in the profile they had been working on received a new, lower priority and more general wording—the revised statement referred to "others in the community" rather than specifically naming the Puerto Rican residents. The bishop said later he

rejected their preliminary profile and sent it back to them. The issue of the Puerto Ricans in the area was not sufficiently raised. I met with them a second time and raised the Puerto Rican neighborhood issue. They complied and went through all the steps so that they could say they had fulfilled the bishop's request. . . . They played it my way to please the bishop. They had already made up their minds as to whom they were going to call.

The revised profile was sent off to the CDO. Committee members felt they didn't want to wait, passively, for the names from the computer, so they asked the bishop for permission to talk to some clergymen in the interval. When the computer names arrived, the bishop removed most of them from the list he passed on to the calling committee. The vestry decided, in the words of members, to "buck the bishop" and "do their own thing." They invited the Rev. William L. Dove to come to town for an interview, "fell in love with him," and voted unanimously to call him as their next rector.

The consultant described the next events: "The junior warden (also head of the pulpit committee and the real power in the system) called the bishop for an appointment to interview Dove, saying, 'Bishop, we've called a man and we'd like for you to meet him.' After picking himself off the ceiling, the bishop did interview him. Then, on Sunday the past rector preached at St. Luke's and from the pulpit announced that the vestry had called a man."

"I blew my stack," said the bishop. "I vented my anger on Dove. . . . I wrote his bishop about the parish and told him I did not think the charismatic movement would keep the parish alive. It will die in five to ten years. I am not opposed to the charismatic movement. He accepted the call. The Holy Spirit told him to do it. It hurts. It is too late now to go to the neighborhood."

When Jerry Oglethorpe and Bill Whyte made their visit to St. Luke's some months later for retrieval interviews, they found the congregation convinced that their new rector had been "sent by the Lord." Asked if they would make any changes, the reply was a strong no, except that they would establish a stronger Spanish ministry. The consultation was remembered as a helpful event. One member said, "Personally, I think this was a very, very healthy thing for the parish; to think about our purpose and where we are going." The consultant's work was seen as relevant to the calling of the new rector in that it helped clarify the charismatic issue.

But it is clear that the consultation never had a chance to perform the functions for which it was intended, because it was caught between a forceful bishop and a congregation reacting strongly to his interventions. Perhaps the congregation bypassed the vacancy consultation process also because of their feeling that a clergyman should be sent, not chosen. Participants drew learnings from the experience. Oglethorpe noted that "parishes need an opportunity to really 'buy in' and not use consultation as a 'must do' order from the bishop." McInnes had some suggestions for improving vacancy consultations:

The bishop should be extremely supportive of the parish in arranging supply priests . . . to reduce the panic.

If at all possible, the consultant should be brought in prior to the formation of the pulpit or calling committee, to work in the process of the formation of that committee and to work with the vestry on the job description, power, limitations, duties, etc. of that committee.

There should be a set pulpit or calling committee, not a pick-up group with no decision power as I experienced at St. Luke's. This committee should represent all factions of the parish: old, young; men, women; conservative, liberal; etc. The committee should have vestry linkages, but not be a totally controlled committee. Once they make a decision, it should be their responsibility to sell the man to the vestry.

The story of how a new rector came to St. Luke's Church is rich in drama, in human and systematic dynamics, and in learnings for other congregations.

SEVEN

St. Mary's

"I should have gone on a two-month paid vacation while the parish went through the vacancy process."

WHEN Father Dimittis announced his intention of retiring as rector of St. Mary's, the bishop met with the rector; with the assistant, Father John Kirkson; and with the vestry to outline the vacancy process he wanted St. Mary's to follow. He offered names of several possible consultants. Nine members of the vestry volunteered to serve on a selection committee, to which would be added two nonvestry members for balance. The senior warden, Sam Peabody, offered to arrange a meeting with the selected consultant, Bill Graves, in August.

Having outlined a fairly long series of sessions with the selection committee, and receiving Peabody's assurances that the $200-$300 fee for these sessions would present no problem, Graves went to work with the committee. He spelled out goals for the work in simple terms:

"To understand the church well enough so that the vestry can choose the best man for the job; to give the new rector as clear a picture as possible of what the church is like; to define his job and the jobs of the laity."

During the first evening Bill Graves suggested that they try to involve a wider group in the committee's work. But according to his report, they felt that only this group was really concerned and that the others would not come.

As the work progressed, Graves noticed signs of submerged conflict in the committee. As early as the third session he presented a design for surfacing and dealing with the areas of tension. "In my experience," he told the members, "I have found it helpful to a team like this to air tensions early in the process, rather than later on, when we don't have time to air them properly, and when our task is pressing us." The group seemed to respond positively to this suggestion.

For a while conflict management continued to be a central theme of their work together. However, by the fourth session new problems emerged. Angry letters from parishioners expressed distrust of the selection committee, which they said was "closed" and already had made up its mind whether or not to call the assistant as rector. From this point on, the committee made efforts to involve the rest of the congregation through letters, meetings, and a questionnaire, but the atmosphere remained political and tense.

Lines between the pro- and anti-Kirkson factions became more and more clearly drawn as the sessions went on. Graves saw his task as providing a fair hearing for the minority, which happened to be three women who were opposed to calling the assistant. During the final sessions, he also struggled with the question of how much direction he ought to provide for the committee's work. A congregational meeting he had left to the committee to prepare was not well planned, and he concluded: "When I leave the design up to others, something inferior is produced."

After this meeting, Bill provided stronger direction. He took home the committee's final report, which he had been reluctant to criticize during the meeting because of the pressures of time, and expanded it to include more of the work they had done together. Graves now felt time-pressured, recognizing the committee's growing impatience and sense of urgency. "I left the last meeting," he wrote to Loren Mead, "thinking that I would be involved in the process of selection. In fact, the committee handled the selection process without me from that time on. I felt disappointed. . . ."

The next news of St. Mary's comes from the interpretive report of consultants Stanley Littlehouse and Ann Lovington, who visited the parish in May to conduct interviews. The interview team quickly became sympathetic to the plight of new rector John Kirkson and his wife. The former assistant had understood the bishop to say that the vacancy consultation would be completed by the time Father Dimittis left in October, and that Father Kirkson would thereafter become rector. The sessions were, in fact, not over until November, and the two-month hiatus left Kirkson, as priest-in-charge, in an extremely embarrassing situation.

The congregation became increasingly polarized over the question of whether or not to offer him the job he wanted. Members later saw the Kirksons' need for ministry during this period, though they were unaware of this need during the difficult two months. No official announcement of Kirkson's selection had been made, and the new rector refused to plan for his institution until this was done. Kirkson wanted to work out a contract with the vestry, which had agreed to do so, but was now dragging its feet. The consultant had been eased out before the selection and was not now on hand to assist in the negotiations.

The effect of the lack of stated priorities was that Kirkson was "breaking his neck to do everything." Even a strongly anti-Kirkson member admitted that "he had tried lately to please people more." Still another effect of the lack of a contract was that since the DRE had left, Kirkson was now doing the work formerly done by three staff members. The budget would not permit hiring a new assistant, and he had received only a minimal salary increase. Littlehouse and Lovington felt if no one acted on these problems, they would soon "reach the point of no return."

Communication problems dominated the vacancy consultation period. Those who were aware of the selection committee's work (and many were not) saw it as "clergy selection, not parish evaluation." Most felt that an evaluation would be redundant, since a study had been done six months previously at the time Kirkson was hired as assistant. Why go through this complicated, time-consuming, and expensive process of clergy selection, when the parish felt quite ready to decide whether or not to accept the man at hand? This was seen to be the real decision St. Mary's faced, and people supposed that the committee was wrestling with that decision.

Bill Graves's efforts to provide a fair hearing for the minority were seen as his taking sides with the anti-Kirkson faction and were a major reason for the majority's easing him out. Efforts to open the committee's work to the congregation were described as "too little, too late." Littlehouse and Lovington concluded that "consultants must concentrate from the very beginning on helping their clients to seek input from the total system, and to report out often and in many forms."

Despite the problems, several helpful learnings and suggestions came out of the consultation at St. Mary's. Members wondered whether a different process should have been used since they were considering an incumbent clergyman for the rector's job. They felt this process was "an insult to the Kirksons." A member of the selection committee put it gently to Graves: "I really don't think that we at St. Mary's were in a position to make full use of this selection process."

A suggestion was made that some other method be used for choosing the selection committee, one that would not result in a situation that favored carrying old vestry conflicts into the committee. Some of these conflicts, in the case of St. Mary's, seemed eased following the consultation, and there were positive attitudes toward the consultant. Several vestry members traced better group functioning and personal growth to Bill's work with them. But regarding the appropriateness of the vacancy consultation process, it was a little as though the parish had asked, "What time is it?" and received the answer, "Have a banana."

EIGHT

Church of the Resurrection

"We had three old men in a row as our rectors. We were in hopes that Father LeJeune's youthful enthusiasm would rub off on the old bodies around here."

AFTER three years, the doctors had to admit defeat in their struggle to save Father Elton Elder's eyesight. The final operation a failure, Elder announced his retirement as rector of the Church of the Resurrection in Clark's Canyon. The Elders went to stay with Bishop Shephard while Elton waited for a Seeing Eye dog and his wife looked for a job.

Members of the parish had mixed reactions when they heard that Elder was definitely leaving. They had been aware of and sympathetic with his increasing difficulties, and they were not surprised when he decided he could not continue as rector. The two previous rectors had been in ill health, so most parishioners agreed it was time to try a young, healthy rector. Some felt that during the period of the rector's hospitalization "the backbone of the church grew stronger."

Bill Handy, the senior warden, remembers thinking, "What do I do now? Gosh, it's my job to do something, and if there is no guidance it won't be easy." Bishop Shephard arranged a special vestry meeting with Handy for the following week, recording the purposes of the meeting in his log:

1. to push them to organize a responsible fund drive for the seeing eye organization and the Elders;

2. to walk through the diocesan vacancy consultation procedure;

3. to work out with him as senior warden ways I can be pastor to him as pastor of the congregation. . . .

Meeting for lunch with the bishop, vestrymen reported that the parish was "unsettled and uncertain." Many people were disgruntled. Many young families with small children had left. Finances were tight. The bishop expressed his major personal investment in this vacancy consultation. He said that if they could find the right priest in this parish it would mean six years of peace before he retired. So they were not to worry about making demands on his time!

The vestrymen studied the bishop's "Suggested Steps for Calling a Rector," and made plans to interview parishioners after church the following Sunday, using questions from the text:

What are some of the things you think it is important for this parish to do in the next few years?

Indicate your personal opinion of how the parish should spend its money. (A list follows.)

Indicate the value you place on the following possible activities of a rector (checklist follows):

What are the areas of greatest effectiveness in past rectors you would like to see continued?

What special needs do you see in this congregation that might call for special abilities in a rector?

What personal qualities do you believe important in a rector, and how much weight do you attach to each of them?

Vestrymen would visit members who were not present that Sunday, since they and the bishop felt it was important to find out the opinions of people who were unhappy with the parish.

The meeting ended with relieved feelings that a direction had been gained. As the warden said afterward, "I know it's going to be hard work, but now we know where to put in the work. None of us knew how you get a rector except maybe put an ad in the paper."

A calling committee of representatives of parish organizations (including nonexistent organizations like "nonregular church members") was formed and prepared a rough profile from the questionnaires. The committee then met with Bishop Shephard to put the profile in final shape and to fill out the CDO forms. During this work session the bishop found that committee members were having difficulty in keeping up with his changing roles—first as group member, discussing improvements in the profile; next as bishop, adding to the profile his concerns for interchurch cooperation and minority groups in the community. The bishop reported:

When we moved to the CDO form, my role changed again and I said that I would try to act as though I were the stupid computer, making sure they gave me directions that wouldn't let me make mistakes. . . . One of the role problems that I had came from the fact that I've worked with many of the same vestrymen before on finances and diocesan supplements to that congregation. Several times I was asked, "Is this all right?" and I had to say, probably six times, "I've stated what my investments are as bishop; what I'm doing now is to help you be clear about where this parish is and where you want to lead it."

The profile listed the bishop's investments as addenda; its major focus was on finding a priest who would tend to public worship and minister to the needs of the congregation.

A suggestion in the profile was that the new rector needed to help the congregation with its fears of not surviving and its need to move with hope on their mission. These fears had come to a head one night when the bishop gave the committee "a roasting for becoming so ingrown." One member remembered this as the most helpful thing the bishop had done. "He said," she recalled, "we were still hunting for someone to maintain our survival syndrome rather than blossoming out."

Nine days after the profile and CDO forms were put in the mail, the computer print-outs arrived. The bishop sent them, along with additional names that had been suggested, to trusted associates, and asked for reactions. The calling committee interviewed two men and the list was narrowed down to three. The youngest of the three, the Rev. Philippe LeJeune, flew West from St. Louis. He spent an hour with the bishop receiving a briefing on the parish and he visited Clark's Canyon. The senior warden liked the way LeJeune went to businesses in town, talked with people and looked at the community "to get an overall picture." All were impressed with his efforts. They tried to be frank, telling him about the good and bad factors. LeJeune felt pressed for time: "There was a lot riding on that one interview, both ways, and a lot to be done in a short time."

The vestry voted eleven to one to call Father LeJeune, and on September 15 the new rector telephoned Bishop Shephard that he had accepted. The bishop wrote: "The Church of the Resurrection should be congratulated in being able to move in four months from announcement of vacancy to filling of vacancy. That's fairly close to record time. I know you must be relieved."

Looking back on his decision, LeJeune said, "There were some major factors that impressed me to come here—their willingness to admit difficulties, frankly. They did not bring me here under false pretenses. . . . Bishop Shephard's personality and knowing him were infinite assets and influenced me strongly."

Before Christmas, the bishop met again with the vestry and new rector to evaluate the consultation, "to rethink the profile . . . and work through similarities and differences between his perception and theirs." Bill Handy posted the questions used the previous June, with the members' replies in red and the new rector's in blue.

Bishop Shephard's log for the period reads:

We identified six areas in which both priest and people were in substantial agreement. The vestry at that point took kindly to my suggestion that the rector, before the next vestry meeting, write out a proposal of what he would like to accomplish on those six in the next twelve months and work out an agreement with them to accomplish those things. . . . At the end of twelve months, they plan to meet for an accountability session to see how well they've done.

Comments on the vacancy procedure included a number of criticisms of the CDO print-outs as hard to read, and positive evaluations of the bishop's consultation. This one is typical: "It was the first time I ever felt that I had a real voice in the selection of a priest, even though I had been on a vestry several times before when we called one."

When Mary Lou FitzSimmons visited Clark's Canyon in June to conduct interviews for Project Test Pattern, she found parishioners pleased with the results of the consultation. One interviewee said: "A unique quality was that he had been born in France. We had become so ingrown that we wouldn't even recognize the church in the next town. Some perspective!" Both LeJeune and vestry members hoped that as time went on the new rector would have to spend less time on administration, which was receiving more time than seemed justified.

Some suggestions were made to improve the consultative process. Bill Handy had been forced to carry too much of the load during the vacancy period. LeJeune felt it would have been better to have visited the parish before talking with the bishop. More computer complaints were forthcoming: "By the time you go through ten of those print-outs, the whole thing is garbled."

However, the new rector felt positive about the bishop's role, telling Mary Lou FitzSimmons, "It is my understanding that he had a great concern as an extension of his ministry to get data and improve the process by which rectors were called." Another comment by LeJeune suggested that he was not confident of the reliability of the data gathered during the consultation: "When the congregation filled out the thirty-question expectation chart it meant one thing. If they filled it out a second time, they would probably fill it out differently."

One member summed up many of the parishioners' feelings: "The bishop was encouraging. Our morale was low. He was firm and understanding. Remember how we felt just a year ago compared to the way we're feeling tonight?"

NINE

Church of St. Barnabas

"A word of advice: if you develop the kind of leadership we have, you could function forever without a minister."

THE Church of St. Barnabas, begun as a mission in a middle-class suburb in 1957, was losing the third clergyman in its short history. Responding to the offer of a tempting and appropriate position, the Rev. Don Robertson announced his resignation. The parish responded with grief, understanding, and self-confidence:

It was like a death.

I never saw so many tears. But we were cocksure we could do it ourselves.

He made us strong, and while sad, we were glad for his opportunity.

Bishop Webster remembered that the parishioners' first thought was, "How can we get another Don?" Characteristically, this independent congregation was confident of its ability to handle problems on its own. It immediately appointed a Searchers' Committee, made up of eager volunteers, which began producing a booklet on the parish. After the committee's work was under way, Bishop Webster suggested to the wardens that they take some time over the calling process, get clear about the nature of their own parish and its needs, and make use of diocesan staff consultant Larry Durrell.

The April parish newsletter reported that the committee decided to work with the consultant; the implication was they could do it on their own, but if professional help was available, why not make use of it? After meeting with Durrell, the Searchers' Committee sent a letter to the parish describing two forthcoming parish meetings: "On the first evening you will have an opportunity to express your concerns and your hopes for this parish. On the second evening we will report the results of the previous meeting and ask you to help us rank our most pressing needs." Following the first evening, Durrell reported his impression that this was a solid, enthusiastic group, clearly well led by the former rector and possessing strong lay initiative and leadership.

At the second meeting, some group leaders protested that "the design was too hard . . . we are a freewheeling discussion group parish and this is too organized." From data generated from the parish meetings, the Searchers' Committee worked to produce a profile including sections on the church's self-image and the type of man they wanted for the job. The bishop felt "they developed a parish profile which was a pretty accurate perception of the parish. They wanted someone who would support lay participation. They were able to develop clear criteria for the Clergy Deployment Office."

The committee wrote in the profile:

Having grown from a priest-centered parish where the laity relied on being told what to do, we have now arrived at the point where we like sharing leadership and responsibility with the rector in a cooperative partnership arrangement. This "maturing" on the part of the laity has just developed over the past several years and needs to be nurtured and further encouraged. We've been shown what we *can* do and we like it!

Committee members knew that the type of man they had described was heavily influenced by Don Robertson. One commented in a retrieval interview: "We drew up a profile just a slight bit below [the new rector]—if the water was a little muddy he could walk on it. In some ways it was too idealistic —we knew it was too much."

From profile-writing the committee went on to training for, arranging, and conducting interviews with the candidates whose names were produced by the CDO computer. The July newsletter describes the committee's concerns at this stage:

What questions would best get at those issues the parish had stated were most important to us?

How could various [interviewing] teams compare results?

How would we decide which men to consider further?

After four months of work, the committee was ready to send four candidates' names to the vestry. In spite of some concerns about the amount of time the process was taking and the occasional feeling of being bogged down in details, the Searchers' Committee had pride and satisfaction in their work. The vestry's first-choice candidate sent the parish a tape recording that was enthusiastically received, and Bob Donaldson became St. Barnabas's next rector. A suggestion was made that tape recordings be more widely used by candidates as an initial communication with the parish.

The congregation seems happy with its choice. "He's a good guy—we really like him," said one young member. Bishop Webster was pleased: "He has an open style—flexible, innovative and imaginative. He respects the lay participation criteria." Plans for regular mutual evaluation were made, though there was ambivalence about this. "We shouldn't make him account for his time. He's an adult—we chose him carefully," said one member.

Most people had positive feelings about the vacancy consultation period, and, according to the bishop, "Larry Durrell liked St. Barnabas's spirit and attitude and said the consultation had gone easily." Durrell saw the seven-month consultation period as a positive feature because it gave parishioners "time to grieve." Members seemed to feel Durrell's work had been helpful, though not essential. Typical comments were:

"I don't think he helped in the long run outcome, but it was good help in adding cohesiveness to the effort."

"I thought our approach was good, but we appreciated his help."

The consultant was seen as helpful in involving the whole parish in the process: "Every person could have a finger in the pie," and one parishioner saw the consultative process as valuable in forging a new link with the diocese. But another member remembered an incident that offended her: "We had been asked to be prompt and Durrell was late. He threw his briefcase on the desk and put his feet up on the desk"—which had been kept "reverently" empty.

The freedom of St. Barnabas's people to criticize the consultant seemed a consequence of their strength and independence. Professional leadership was both something they could use and do without.

The vacancy period at St. Barnabas illustrates the unique quality of this experience for a congregation that is strong, independent, and capable of dealing with its feelings in a direct, open, and productive way.

TEN

The Trout Lake Missions

"The bishop was direct and laid it all on the table. He told us that we had two ways to go—to spend our time crying, or to get on our feet and work toward keeping the congregation alive and get a new vicar. He was not superior in any way; he was just one of us and interested in us. He was firm, though."

BISHOP Bunyan was camping with two of his sons on Trout Lake when he heard that Father Stoughton's heart condition was causing him increasing pain. When the bishop hiked over to the vicarage at Otter Gap, on the north side of the lake, he found that the vicar was hoping a new clergyman could be found soon to take over the missions at Otter Gap and Hatchery Dam, the latter forty miles up the mountain. The bishop noticed as he walked back that the area around Trout Lake was one of the most beautiful parts of the diocese, and there were signs that it was becoming a popular place for vacations. The gold mines were closing down; most of the people were dependent for their livelihoods on logging, the railroad, the Forest Service, mink farming, and recreation.

Returning to his office on Monday morning, the bishop found that the assistant at St. Michael's Church in Pines, thirty miles south of Trout Lake, was also leaving. Three churches needed men—and the bishop knew it would not be possible to pay more than one man to serve all of them. As he had done a dozen times in the past year, the bishop began working as vacancy consultant in his diocese.

The people at Otter Gap and Hatchery Dam had been without a clergyman for several years before Father Stoughton's arrival. It was important to both that their own churches stay alive, but each congregation was aware of the state of the diocesan budget and afraid that the bishop might have to close down one of the missions. When they heard that Father Stoughton was leaving, one mission member "felt that the end of the world had come." Another said, "The word I would use is 'waiting,' waiting to see what's going to happen—a kind of limbo."

The bishop visited the missions the following week and talked to each one in a candid manner. He brought guidelines for the work that would need to be done: "A parish in search of a priest must first go in search of itself." He also left a questionnaire designed to reveal congregational needs, priorities and strengths, and some description of the congregation. Over thirty-six responses were received. Members studied the bishop's guidelines:

What will you be looking for? An old legend with too much truth in it says, "A walking collection of all the virtues." More seriously, the prime ingredients are obvious enough: faithfulness to God, and to the Church and his role within it; priestcraft, knowledge of his job; openness to both new and old ideas; ability to relate to people, at home as well as within the parish; compassion without sentimentalism; some skill, not only verbal, in communications; and a reasonable self-discipline both at work and in his private life, especially in handling money.

Members of the missions at Otter Gap and Hatchery Dam were realistic: "We'd take the best of those available since we're a place this size. We had to recognize our limits and couldn't expect to get someone like the bishop." Bishop Bunyan helped them summarize the results of their work in a profile, which read, in part:

The combination of responsibility for two missions in towns with their own particular style, plus ministering in a larger community an hour away, places real demands upon a priest. He must be well disciplined in the use of his time and personally capable of standing in the middle of the pull between the three points, plus that of his personal and family life. Advantages in this very fact are the excitement that comes from the diversity and a form of team ministry relationship with the rector of St. Michael's Church.

With the widely spread responsibilities of this multiple post, the people did not want a clergyman who would spread himself too thin; they wanted a clergyman to tend the churches and concentrate on pastoral work. Working on the self-study and the profile, with Bishop Bunyan's help, gave the members "a sense of direction and a way of accepting responsibility."

After the profile had been sent to "the great computer back East," the bishop's help was still needed at Trout Lake. One of the problems that depressed mission members was the fact that so many members were behind in their pledges. On his next visit, the bishop, deeply concerned about the missions' dwindling income, offered, and his offer was eagerly accepted, to do a kind of stewardship program that evening.

As this work progressed, it became evident that an internal struggle was taking place between the "in group" and the "out group." The latter was composed of a few long-time residents "who carry a heck of a lot of weight around town," the bishop reported. This group had been opposed all along to going through the vacancy procedures: "Just let the bishop send us a vicar," they urged.

The bishop wrote in his report that "the committee, after having tested me as to what their authority was, took a formal vote and decided that they were going to follow the guidelines and to heck with anybody else. There seemed to be a real relief at this point, that it was all right for them to use their power."

The bishop shared with the Trout Lake people his idea that during a vacancy period, the out group started having some sense of hope that the situation could change. This theory "rang bells all over the place, and it seemed to relieve them greatly to know that they were feeling pain but it was normal." During subsequent retrieval interviews, one member remembered that "we got into a family fight," and that "the bishop just listened and let it all come out. It had to anyway, and folks needed to be heard out."

The following month, December, the bishop wrote in his report:

I volunteered to take the Christmas Eve services at Otter Gap and Hatchery Dam, partly from the desire to protect other priests from having to handle a long, hard trip, but more, I believe, to reinforce particularly at Otter Gap the sense that I really do care for them and can, in fact, act for their interest instead of for my own schemes. As bishop, I've pushed both congregations fairly hard on their financing, and I've had some feedback that a few of the people, at any rate, translate this into the bishop trying to get money for his own pet projects or at least bleeding them unmercifully.

In January three names arrived from the computer. The committee studied the print-outs with some difficulty. As one member later reported, "The computer information wasn't really helpful because it lacked the kind of personal information we needed." Only one man seemed a possible candidate.

The bishop, at a regional conference, received information that strongly indicated this candidate would not be the right person for the Trout Lake missions and the post at St. Michael's. At the same time, Bishop Bunyan realized that the shrinking income at two other small missions in the diocese meant that they would have to share a clergyman and that the Rev. William Pruitt would be out of a job. Bill Pruitt read the Trout Lake profile, and both he and the bishop felt that it described an appropriate field for his interests and abilities.

Pruitt visited Otter Gap, Hatchery Dam, and St. Michael's, was accepted by the committee, and together they worked out a contract. It specified that the tiny vicarage at Hatchery Dam would continue to be rented, and the house next to the church at Otter Gap would be prepared for the Pruitts. Forty percent of Bill's salary would be paid by Otter Gap, twenty-five percent by Hatchery Dam, and thirty-five percent by St. Michael's; Otter Gap paid the largest percentage because they had the privilege of a resident vicar. "No matter where you live," said Bill, "the other places feel that you are leaving them out a little bit—the other community is always going to feel like the tail on the dog."

The churches were delighted that Bill Pruitt was coming, but Bishop Bunyan was left with mixed feelings about the Trout Lake placement. He had hoped to provide the missions with freedom of choice as well as with a solution to financial problems. But all the hard work to study the missions and draw up a profile had resulted in what felt like an episcopal appointment. He looked forward to some feedback from Ron Lewis and Betsy Parsons, who were going to Trout Lake to conduct retrieval interviews for PTP, and then there would be his own evaluation session with the Trout Lake churches and their new vicar three months after Pruitt's arrival.

At the evaluation, wrote the bishop,

The question will be what was useful and what could be improved in the bishop's work with the priest and the committee in this particular placement? I do this, first of all, to legitimatize evaluation. . . . The second question has to do with, given your expectations as parish leaders, how has this particular priest been meeting them? The other question is to the priest—given your understanding of these congregations before you came, what has surprised you?

This evaluation would not take place till the summer, since it had been agreed that Pruitt would not leave his present mission until Easter.

In the absence of the new vicar, therefore, the PTP interviews centered around the bishop's work as vacancy consultant. Members' comments reflected gratitude for his helping them move toward taking increased responsibility for their churches' lives:

I think if there had been objections to Father Pruitt's coming here, he wouldn't be coming.

It's hard to put my finger on it, but the bishop was not above us. He was just like part of the group, accepting all the problems.

He was genuine, encouraging, and always followed through. It was good to look at ourselves and examine together where we wanted to go.

The thing I most remember about what he did was to come down here and spend a great deal of time with all of us, and more or less arrange interviews with everybody concerned. He explained things, laying them out on the table where you could see them, and let you make your own decisions about them.

ELEVEN

Grace Church

"The consultation got the congregation thinking. We have a lot of old people. We were just sitting back, 'keeping the rail clean.' We had plenty of money, but as I see it now, we weren't doing anything. We just coasted for a long time."

CONSULTANT Royall Rogers described Grace Church in his report as "the oldest Episcopal Church in the diocese . . . the seat of the old families in town . . . a very dignified and staid congregation. The people are happy with their life style, pleased with their beautiful old buildings, and deeply aware of the historic roots which feed their lives."

But their rector, the Rev. Lowell Hodgkins, had announced his intention of leaving Grace Church for the second time that year. The first announcement resulted in conversations with a diocesan consultant, a raise in salary, and Hodgkins's agreement to stay on for a while. The second announcement was accepted as final; and parishioners responded to it in different ways.

Hodgkins had been close to some of the older and wealthier members of the congregation, and all but the *most* conservative of this group were sorry to lose their rector. (One member had left the church because the rector felt he had to go along with national church policies, such as membership in the National Council of Churches.) A member of the group to which the rector had ministered said later, "I was sad—I wondered why he was leaving; I wondered if we hadn't done something he wanted us to do."

Other parishioners saw Hodgkins as alienated from younger members and unwilling to support lay leadership or programs of outreach. On the whole, no one expressed any strong reactions of grief. One member said, "I was close to Lowell, sorry to see him go. But also, I felt we could turn his leaving into a new beginning."

The senior warden invited Royall Rogers to come to Grace Church to talk with the vestry about "this new thing the bishop wants us to do." This "new thing" was vacancy consultation, which the bishop recommended for every parish that lost a rector. He suggested Rogers, who had arranged with his small parish to have time available for quite a lot of consultative work. The vestry agreed to pay Rogers whatever he asked, to invite the whole parish to a consultative session, and to call the consultant back to help negotiate a contract when the new rector was found.

Rogers called his report on the day at Grace Church "Vacancy Consultation as Life-Style Intervention." The design began with the 11 a.m. Sunday service at which Rogers, dressed in suit and tie, rose to explain vacancy consultation to the congregation. The "life-style intervention" at this point was clear to a young parishioner who reported that "a lot of people left the church that day because Roy Rogers came in with the wildest suit you ever saw." (Another parishioner estimated the number of walkers-out as three.) Morning Prayer continued, with a sermon about God calling comfortable people to move in new directions, and a statement that "Lowell Hodgkins has left Grace Church, and things will never be the same again."

Small groups moved into the parish hall to talk about "what

I want this church to be for me and for others." Roy and his wife, Rita, collated and mimeographed these data during the afternoon and posted areas of concern on newsprint. Eighty parishioners returned in the evening to continue working in interest groups. At the end of the evening, Roy and Rita held a dialogue in the presence of the parishioners, making observations and telling how they felt about the day's work. They noted with concern that almost no one under forty years of age had come to the meeting. They further wondered aloud if the congregation's concern for continuity did not contradict its strong desire for things to stay the same.

Both the reluctance to change and the concern about involving younger people were evident in the data. A typical comment described the desired clergyman as a "youth-oriented, conservative man of God." Outreach tended to be seen as efforts to make newcomers welcome. The parish's mission was summarized by one member as: "Continue the beauty and dignity of Grace Church." The conflict between the congregation's major concerns was seen by parishioners: "We wanted someone to reach the youth but we didn't want to change." Several members also saw that this lack of consistency made for unrealistic expectations of a future rector. As one old lady put it, "Of course, we wanted a saint to fall out of the sky—guess he would have been lonesome." Or, as another humorist put it: "We wanted a thirty-year-old ex-Confederate general."

The day had been fun, people had enjoyed the Rogerses' designs for helping people get involved with each other, and the "life-style intervention" seemed to have been a success for those who attended. Rogers reported: "It had more of the flavor of play than of work. The work of finding a minister is yet to be done. The hard questions about whether or not the younger generation and the nonfamily people are going to be let into the decision-making in this congregation have not been answered."

The calling committee, whose membership was identical with the fifteen-member vestry, interviewed a number of clergymen. They narrowed the list to three candidates and struggled to make a decision. Some were disturbed by the fact that one of three men at the top of the list had been involved in a garbage strike. Conservatives and moderates reached a compromise and agreed to call the Rev. Rufus Young as their next rector. According to one committee member, "Rufus just seemed to fit. He is a fairly conservative, energetic young family man."

Committee members did not agree to what extent the data had been useful to them in reaching their decision, but they did give the material from the consultation to the candidates. Rufus Young found it useful "because we both wanted much the same things, with one exception—their data called for no change. The data helped me look at the parish more realistically. It was quite different from my past experience of the soft sell at the time of calling. It was helpful to me to look at both strengths and weaknesses." Rogers was called back, as had been agreed, to help the new rector and his vestry negotiate a contract.

Retrieval interviews showed a high level of enthusiasm for the new rector, mainly because of his priorities of involving and improving communications among people, especially youth. After Young entertained sixty younger members at the rectory, two parishioners reported the number as two hundred. One woman who was impressed by his tact and care in introducing changes reported: "At the United Thank Offering presentation service we have always worn veils. This year he changed it in a very nice way. To my surprise, many agreed with him. Rufus explained that he wanted to unveil all our activities and have real openness together."

One politically minded vestryman challenged his fellows: "I'll bet you conservatives that you will be changing more with this man than with a liberal. If my man had come you would not have cooperated with him—probably blocked him. But I'll get a lot of what I want; you'll go with this man because he is a conservative."

Young reported his one difficulty was with Hodgkins: "In a five-week period the former rector has returned four times, three of these for sacramental actions. This makes it very difficult to terminate one ministry and for me to begin another here at Grace Church."

In retrospect, the vacancy period was seen as a positive event in the parish's history, as illustrated by the following comments at retrieval interviews:

The church came closer together, people shouldered more responsibility, everyone got along better together.

In fact, the bishop said it scared him, the church going so well without a minister.

Many people were impressed with the calling procedure as involving a large number of parishioners and more calling committee members than had previously been the custom. There was a feeling that communications between committee and parish were clear; and that the lack of secrecy and the total parish involvement gave the congregation a sense of ownership of the decision-making process. One respondent criticized the calling committee for asking the bishop for recommendations: "I would not ask bishops for names. Bishops are human; they want to move certain people." It was not clear that anything in the respondent's vacancy consultation experience had precipitated his criticism.

Several members felt the important thing about the Sunday with the Rogerses was the way it helped the parish look at itself and come to a realization of the kind of leadership it needed. "What I thought was important," said one, "was the doing, the action, the process—that's what was important. The report could have been thrown in the trash can." Some members looked forward to doing it again:

I think it would be great to come together in a meeting with the Rogerses, every couple of years.

It is exciting to think about doing an evaluation with outside, objective people.

Someone trained as well as objective—it would be great.

TWELVE

St. Andrew's

"In the process of getting the man out, we cut up some of our family."

BISHOP John Hillman, who had volunteered to participate in the Vacancy Consultation Project, reported to Project Test Pattern that storm warnings at St. Andrew's had erupted into a gale. The rector, Samuel Titus, was leaving.

The rector of St. Andrew's for the past decade had been a "by the book" sort of guy, with little imagination, who sees the Church as something involving services, placidity and paying the bills. . . . A year ago, I got wind of a "dust-up," led primarily by four vestrymen who were concerned about the lack of movement in the parish and the seeming unwillingness of the rector to work for change. I offered my services to see if we could open up the issue, but the attitude of the rector was that if they wanted some changes in program, mission, etc., they were an unrepresentative minority.

The new senior warden, in an attempt to heal the breach, invited the bishop to meet with the rector and vestry. The rector refused to attend the meeting, and shortly thereafter his resignation was requested and submitted. "Apparently," wrote the bishop, "the 'antis' decided that it would be better to blow the gaff completely than to die slowly of spiritual gangrene."

Both the bishop and Tom Angstrom, the senior warden, felt inwardly torn. Angstrom felt it was his duty to stand behind the rector. "I was going to be loyal to him even if I didn't agree with him," he recalled in a retrieval interview. "I was against the way they did it. I felt crushed, decapitated." The bishop, while sympathetic with parish members who wanted to work for change, found himself having to be pastor to both the clergyman and the congregation. "I believe," wrote the bishop, "that I have credibility with folk on both sides of the issue, although I find that my style of being a bishop and offering services and making decisions is not the authoritative one which this clergyman might desire." Titus viewed with impatience the bishop's attempts to place him in another mission in the diocese. He felt that the bishop had the authority to place a man in missions without the congregation's acting in the decision.

Parishioners expressed less reaction to the clergyman's departure than to the split it caused in the parish. Several members left the church, and the breach would not be easy to heal.

The bishop's offer of consultative help had been accepted by the parish, and he attended Titus's last vestry meeting to describe the kind of help he could offer. Hillman reported:

The departing rector led the first part of the meeting, at which there was a great deal of hostility expressed between the senior warden and the treasurer and one or two others. The clergyman left following the first part of the meeting, which he controlled in terms of doing all the reporting. . . . It is this exclusiveness of ministry which, apparently, is the root cause of the conflict here. He announced that the following Sunday would be his last in the church and that he loved them all—said in a way which really meant, I think, "To hell with you!"

After the minister left the vestry meeting, the bishop took the chair, and the meeting became calmer. Vestry members expressed their feelings and heard the bishop's plans for the consultation. They seemed to respond hopefully to a process that promised to involve a large number of parishioners. Bishop Hillman had positive feelings about their first visit:

I think that the tension levels went down while I was there; fundamentally, I felt there was a feeling that they could trust me to do the best possible for them, although they heard me, I hope, when I said that this would probably take time because of the deep conflict in the parish and the need for reconciliation. The new model for consultation, developed by Jim Worth, diocesan director of parish development, Bill Eaglesman, who is new in the diocese, and myself, was aimed particularly at their conflict and recognition that they had to be freed to express their conflicts, guilts, reconciliation, etc.

Bishop Hillman closed his report with the confession that he already had a number of promising candidates in mind for St. Andrew's, and was "tempted to say, 'Let me do it for you, gang—here's the man.' Bite my tongue, however!"

A letter from the bishop to the congregation spoke of the possibilities of the vacancy period:

Whenever there is a vacancy in the ordained leadership of a congregation, that limb of the Body of Christ has a real opportunity to move, with excitement and joy, into new understandings of mission and ministry. . . .

Arriving at a new rector's place, believe it or not, is much like getting married. It is not done inadvisedly or lightly, but reverently, discreetly, honestly, soberly and in the awe of God.

Enclosed in the bishop's letter was a questionnaire designed to discover parishioners' concerns for St. Andrew's ministry and their ideas about what parts of that ministry should be "hired out" to a clergyman. Plans were announced for a parish meeting, at which a search committee would be appointed, and a two-day training consultation with the search committee and vestry.

At the annual parish meeting, fifty members volunteered to work on the search committee. Fourteen members, chosen to represent as many groups and factions as possible, were selected. A "man with no enemies" was appointed chairman. During the retrieval interviews, one search committee member saw the committee's selection as an attempt to deal with "a definite division of opinion. In our search it was very important that we accept that. As a result we had a larger search committee than necessary to ensure wide representation."

Two weeks later, Worth and Eaglesman helped the committee and vestry wrestle with fundamental questions: What is the ministry of this parish? How can we accomplish this ministry? What part of this ministry do we want hired to be done? They explored the current situation in the parish, its origins in the past, and its possibilities for the future. The training sessions concluded the consultative phase of the vacancy period, which was remembered as important by the committee members: "Two representatives from the bishop helped us get started in the right direction."

The committee began its work by correlating the questionnaires. The low percentage returned was attributed by one member to the split over the rector's departure. Comments on the returned forms reflected a focus on this issue:

We need to enlist the support of the entire church in selection of a new rector.

Many rejoice while many are sick at heart—a seemingly insurmountable situation. Will the church be reunited? We are certain that it will!

It is my feeling that anyone who doesn't have to answer for his actions is apt to fall into the natural pattern of doing as *he pleases,* knowing full well that no one can even question his actions.

Is it not possible to hire a rector on a year-to-year basis? At the end of each year, assess the performance of the rector and set new goals for the coming year. This type of arrangement would not only assist the rector in his work but would of necessity force the vestry to do some thinking about the performance of the past year and set new goals for themselves for the new year.

The profile the search committee constructed from the questionnaire data listed pastoral care as the first priority:

At present the parish is divided into two factions. Our greatest need and first goal will be to reunite these two factions. This will be the responsibility of both the priest and the congregation. Poor communications have contributed greatly to this division. Better communications among the entire parish family are essential. A yearly evaluation session will be expected.

The bishop watched the committee's progress from a distance, remarking that while a number of people had left the parish "the Gideon's army that is left is enthusiastic and active, and attendance at all things is growing." The profile completed and the request form submitted to the Clergy Deployment Office, Bishop Hillman met with the committee to give them his list of candidates. Copies of the profile were sent to the candidates on the list, the CDO candidates, and clergymen whose names had been submitted in other ways.

From eight interested respondents, three men were picked for interviews. Bishop Hillman noticed at this point in the proceedings "a certain 'inferiority sense' in our people which is revealed in their doubt that really good and potentially great priests will come to them. They have had a plethora of experience with the less than good." The committee was candid about the parish situation with the three clergymen selected. A call was issued to and accepted by the Rev. Harry McMillan, whose name had come from the CDO, to become St. Andrew's new rector. The bishop was pleased: "I think he will bring good stuff to the diocese and, again, I believe that the search process worked well."

Shortly after McMillan's arrival at St. Andrew's, Sunny Eberhart visited the parish to conduct retrieval interviews. Members felt McMillan had been a good choice, and they were clear about his priorities. Concerns for accountability had risen out of the parish's experience with the former rector. This had resulted in plans for annual evaluation that were clear to priest and people. Search committee members commented:

"A yearly evaluation session means that we won't have problems of communication that we had in the past."

"This evaluation sounds almost like a vote each year—that could be shattering."

The new rector noted: "We'll set goals annually. "We're to recontract on an annual basis, I think—but I'm not worried. I'm impressed with the idea of a yearly evaluation."

Looking back on the vacancy period, most respondents had positive feelings. The bishop's efforts in setting up the process were seen as helpful. It had involved, people remembered, "quite a lot of soul searching." While the bishop and his consultant team had started them thinking, search committee members were clear that they had gone from there on their own. Communicating the committee's progress to the parish was remembered as a problem, though efforts had been made to issue announcements and letters. The fellowship and "beautiful closeness" of the committee as it worked were remembered warmly. Even a parishioner who was less than enthusiastic about the vacancy procedures said, "I don't care for the process. But a larger team picks a man and will support him. The old way was better—the bishop knows the parish and the men. But, in a way, they have gotten what they wanted." Another member noted that "the search committee and vestry have an ego stake" in the new minister.

McMillan felt there was "still a long way to go" in binding up the parish's wounds. Sunny Eberhart, summing up the St. Andrew's situation in her report, agreed:

It was at a breaking situation with the previous rector and now the new, young, attractive, capable rector is being talked about as "that wonderful Father Harry." In the midst of all this joy there are still five people who are very much detached from the parish church. . . . This parish has everything going for it and can be a great parish. At the present time it's very much looking in, as it should, considering its past history.

THIRTEEN

Church of the Holy Communion

"Royall Rogers is definitely not for our church. He's not used to our services. However, he is not, as some have said, the Devil."

THE Rev. Benjamin Praise, known and respected for his teaching ministry, resigned as rector of the Church of the Holy Communion. The resignation came about six months after an altercation with the vestry. This argument had apparently been worked out in the rector's favor, though not without a few residual hard feelings. About half the parishioners were as enthusiastic about the charismatic movement as was their departing rector and were sorry or angry on learning of his resignation. But the major feeling was that he had taught them everything he could and that his talents were badly needed in the parish to which he was going. One parishioner said he "was not unhappy to see him go, because God decided he was needed elsewhere." Grief reactions were also mitigated by some resentment at the amount of time the rector had spent on extraparochial teaching missions, and by a conviction that Father Praise had prepared the laity to go on without his leadership. "He taught us to stand on our own," said one member. "We weren't helpless without a priest." Though some worried about how long they would be leaderless, others were surprised at the participation and hard work done by parishioners.

The chairman of the calling committee, appointed by the vestry, selected committee members from various parish groups. He started to work discreetly, telling committee members "to mingle with people first and talk, and come back with significant information." But his failure to announce the names of committee members created some dissension, forcing him to call open meetings.

The first name offered to the calling committee by the bishop was that of the Rev. Jeffrey Patten. He said, when sounded out by the committee, that it was too soon to leave his present parish. More names were obtained, and another man turned down a call. By this time the calling committee was willing to entertain the bishop's suggestion that Holy Communion enter into a vacancy consultation. The bishop offered them the choice of two diocesan consultants or Royall Rogers. Rogers's work in vacancy consultations in another diocese had reached the bishop's ears, and he would soon be attending a conference in a nearby town. They decided to ask Rogers and his wife to conduct a vacancy consultation at Holy Communion.

Rogers reported to Project Test Pattern that he and Rita used the same design at Holy Communion that they had used earlier at Grace Church. On the date of the report the results were not yet known. But they did have a contract to negotiate the working agreement between congregation and clergyman, when a suitable man was found. Rogers described how leadership patterns established earlier made it difficult for the congregation to work collaboratively with the consultant to solve their problem:

This congregation's dependency problems with relationship to authority are not only deeply rooted, but they are also theologically undergirded. The past rector was very much a "Holy Spirit Man," and the congregation is more oriented to prayer and program than to data gathering and planning. Some vestrymen expected us to (a) gather data; (b) analyze the data; (c) project for them a profile of the man they wanted; and (d) tell them how to find him! Needless to say, they were disappointed in our services.

The congregation also tended to try to give the consultants what they wanted. We countered this by setting them to work formulating their own questions for the evening session instead of having the consultants pose the questions. This, by the way, really worked, and once they got on their own, they really got with each other. In fact they didn't want to go home at 9:30 p.m., the appointed witching hour.

The calling committee, in spite of their distaste for the consultants' style and their resentment of the amount of work that was being left to the committee, did manage to type the data from the consultation and add an introductory comment:

We feel that this report represents a composite picture of the feelings of the congregation towards the talents needed of the next priest called to the Church of the Holy Communion. We feel that the need of a spirit-filled priest is of primary importance.

The committee chairman, who was "getting a lot of flack about the consultation" and experiencing general difficulties in his role as chairman, turned the leadership of the committee over to John Fitzroy. The new chairman described his experience at a prayer mission led by the Rev. Keith Barwell, a popular leader in the charismatic movement: "I went to the rail and asked Keith Barwell for guidance in finding a priest. The next night in the session two friends of Jeff Patten's came in and said Jeff was now available. I felt this was the work of God, a revelation."

Patten at this time was separated from his wife and contemplating divorce. If the uncertainty of his marital situation did not prevent their extending a call, he was willing to accept such a call. The calling committee sent Patten the data from the vacancy consultation, and he brought his copy of the report to a committee meeting covered with comments and challenging questions. The call was extended and accepted. Parishioners later reported to PTP retrieval interviewers Barnaby Stubbs and Frances Potter: "Since that time, Patten and his wife have had a miraculous reconciliation."

Retrieval interviews seemed to indicate a high degree of satisfaction with the new rector. One parishioner summed it up this way: "I think Father Patten is the answer to the prayers of the majority. He is energetic, religious, available, very knowledgeable and deeply spiritual." Some members were a little surprised by the many communion services he conducted. The organist said she "learned right away the Episcopal Church has an awful lot of services."

Many saw their new priest as open, accessible, and busy keeping the home fires burning. One parishioner shook his head: "I think he works too long and too hard; he must earn about a dollar an hour." Patten seemed to enjoy calling, unlike the previous rector.

Both rector and people seemed resistant to the idea of setting priorities for the pastor's work. "I don't know about his priorities," said one member. "He is doing a good job; if he doesn't do a good job, we will know." The rector said, "I haven't actually set priorities. My accountability is to the Lord at present."

There were no plans to negotiate a contract. One interviewee remembered, "We were supposed to have him [Rogers] come when we got a priest and help us set that up. After that day we said we are through with Roy Rogers." Even if Rogers had not offended so many at Holy Communion, it seems doubtful whether the parish would have been interested in a contract—the whole idea of a contract seemed foreign to their mind-set.

As Rogers had anticipated, there were complaints that he had left without correlating any of the material. A minority opinion was submitted by one young member: "The calling committee leaned back in their seats and waited for the consultants to give us a pattern of attack. It slowed down the process a great deal." There were also complaints that the Rogerses "treated us like a bunch of little children," particularly when they closed the consultation with a summarizing dialogue from either side of the room.

But what really "raised the hackles" was the way Rogers had begun the consultation in church with a service—and a service totally unlike anything they had ever seen. No language was too strong to express their disapproval of that service. Members complained about Rogers's lack of dignity in the pulpit, the irreverence of a "fun and games" service, and the fact that Rogers was a "sensitivity priest" rather than a "Holy Spirit priest." Father Patten agreed that opposing dynamics were involved.

There were some positive comments:

He did not give us answers, but he made us think about ourselves. We did learn a lot from the questions.

The information helped us get a man; the material was used.

A number of people here are capable and could have done what Roy did—but the question is, "Would we have done it?"

It sometimes sounded as though members were conscious that the consultation had produced some really good things, but the memory of that service was so distasteful that they didn't want to admit it. This consultation illustrates the difficulty of using collaborative problem-solving methods in a congregation in which a significant subgroup (in this case the charismatics) is more responsive to a directive leadership style. The consultants' insensitivity to the congregation's norms of worship increased the difficulty of communication.

Holy Communion's ambivalence about the consultation seems ironically summed up in the opinion expressed that in reaction to Rogers, members realized how much they had in common, how "together" they were:

Maybe the visit of Royall Rogers was God's way of leading us into this unity. Before his visit we were all at tangents with one another. We had never really looked at ourselves before his visit.

FOURTEEN

St. George's

"Dear Members and Friends of the Parish: For several years, I have been giving serious thought to a career change by leaving the parochial ministry, and plugging into some other area of service. . . ."

BISHOP Brooks Falconer often ran into Angus Goodwin, rector of St. George's, as he walked home from the diocesan offices. Recently the bishop had been struck by Goodwin's "obvious depression and hang-dog demeanor." For ten years the rector had impressed Falconer as a person and as "a good and faithful pastor," but something was obviously very wrong.

After calling Angus into his office for a talk, the bishop concluded that Goodwin wanted to work with people but that he had difficulty making administrative decisions. Goodwin, after his talk with the bishop and after counsel from other sources, resigned from the parish. In his resignation letter he noted that changes in the ministry had lessened his enthusiasm. He felt, he wrote, that the programs of the church seemed no longer relevant to people who were really hurting. He wrote that he would work on a farm for a year or two and would use the time to discover a new direction for his ministry.

Bishop Falconer attended the vestry meeting at which the rector's letter of resignation was presented and told the vestry he thought Angus "had made a reasoned decision, after much consultation." The bishop recommended a vacancy procedure including the appointment of a search committee, the development of a parish profile and job analysis, followed by the examination of a list of candidates, and finally the selection of a new rector. The bishop offered his own services in the parish one weekend each month during the vacancy period, as well as the services of diocesan consultants Lew Kelly and Carl Montobello, in initiating the search process. Above all, the bishop stressed it was important not to hurry; "it was more important to fit the right man to the right job at the right time."

Two days later the bishop wrote to the people of St. George's to inform them of their role in the selection process. An "expectation form" was enclosed with the bishop's letter so that parishioners could decide what activities and qualities in their prospective rector they "deem to be significant."

The vestry appointed a search committee, representing various groups and points of view in the parish, which spent a Sunday evening with the bishop and the diocesan consultant team. Bishop Falconer reported:

Only forty-plus expectation forms were returned, which indicated an apathy which the search committee localized as the key problem with the church. We spent most of the time on the needs and hopes of the parish. They kept trying to focus on the work of the ministry, and we tried to keep them attuned to the ministry of the parish, of which the clergyman would be a part. I think that it was a helpful session for them, but the three of us felt that it didn't have much depth.

The bishop felt that one problem with the evening might have been that the consultant team's design had not been sufficiently well prepared. Since the diocesan offices were down the street from the church, "we assumed that we knew the situation, which might indicate that it is tougher to do a consultation on somewhat home turf."

The following day, the bishop had lunch with a number of community leaders, including the president of the junior college, the director of the local hospital, the president of the chamber of commerce, and the ministers of local churches, in order to get their ideas about what kind of man was needed as rector of St. George's. The community leaders, all of whom accepted the bishop's invitation, were enthusiastic about the request for their input. They wanted the new rector to be "a responsible community-oriented man." This recommendation conflicted with the parishioners' desire for a man devoted to worship and pastoral care. The bishop's report continued: "We met with the search committee at the end of the day, pointing out this discrepancy, and they will take it into account in the profile."

The search committee went to work on the profile and then requested names of candidates from the bishop, the Clergy Deployment Office, and other sources. Periodic reports on the committee's efforts were circulated to the members through the church bulletin. The parish seemed to be thriving during the vacancy period—attendance was up and lay leaders were coming forward. Using the priorities as a guide, the committee narrowed a list of fifteen names to two promising candidates.

Although efforts were made to submit other names at this point, the committee refused to bypass the agreed-upon process. One unfortunate clergyman who showed up at a search committee meeting was greeted with some hostility. The bishop reported that another priest who telephoned the search committee chairman, asking to be considered, was told that they weren't going to depart from the procedure. The gentleman was irate with the chairman, but he stuck to his guns.

"This raises the question," continued the bishop, "of how to interpret to clergy at large the new processes and systems whereby men receive calls. I think that when dioceses and bishops and other functional systems, such as commissions on ministry, establish a process that is stuck with, the message will be gotten across."

It was difficult for the vestry to make a decision between the two appealing candidates the search committee had chosen from the list. Several votes were taken, with varying results. It seemed, said the bishop, that "they didn't have the capacity to choose between them . . . like a kid caught between two luscious looking candy bars." The decision was finally made, by a majority of one, to call the Rev. Jack Painter as St. George's new rector.

One comment on the evaluation forms had been, "enthusiasm wanted." Janet Merriweather, who came to St. George's to conduct retrieval interviews for PTP, found that enthusiasm was just what they had gotten. She reported, "The new rector there is a 'fireball.' For the past two months he's had volunteer work parties painting the whole place. They worked like dogs and are enchanted with the whole affair." People were very happy with the new rector, concluded Janet.

No written contract had been negotiated, nor had specific plans for periodic evaluation been made. "We talked about a letter of agreement," said Jack Painter. "I've hoped things will be tacit and not have to be written down. I open the door to evaluation at every vestry meeting. They need to have a recourse."

Evaluation of the vacancy procedure by participants in the process was generally positive. They remembered having worked through their feelings about Angus Goodwin's resignation, and there was a comment that "the feelings are pretty well gone by now." There was criticism of the evaluation forms as containing terms that should have been put in simpler language. The bishop and the consultant team were seen as "resource people" who helped them organize the vacancy process. It was clear that the development of the profile and subsequent procedures had been the independent work of the search committee. The new rector had worked with the profile: "They had my print-out and matched it with the profile. They gave me an opportunity to look at the profile and reassess my priorities." Participants in the vacancy process concluded that it, on the whole, had been useful:

It took a lot of soul searching.

It made us take a look at ourselves.

Reflections on the Case Histories

AFTER having lived with this varied collection of parishes for several months, I can almost picture them in my mind as a very mixed group of individual people—tall and short, rich and poor, brave and frightened, sophisticated and simple, truculent or eager to please, red- or shining-eyed. In short, they possess all the richly varied and unique characteristics that make each of us unique.

To look at this mixed bag of churches during the vacancy period is to see into the depths of those congregations' lives at a crucial, open moment. Their past and present stand revealed at that moment, and the future is being determined. The departure of the pastor and the process of selecting a new one represent a moment of crisis in the life of a parish; in meeting that crisis, a congregation shows of what it is made.

The openness of the moment of the minister's departure is an occasion for both freedom and fear. The future is open, and changes will come. "Lowell Hodgkins has left Grace Church, and things will never be the same again," said consultant Rogers from the pulpit. The "out group" begins to stir and to hope that things can be different, noticed Bishop Bunyan. People having become aware that they want their parish to take different directions see the prospect or arrival of a new rector as an opportunity to move in those directions. They look around them and see pews filled with old people; maybe a new, young clergyman will bring young people back to the church. Changes will come. As Bishop Shephard wrote, "No leader ever solves the problems for which he is called because the very fact of the search and his coming has radically changed the situation."

The openness and the freedom inherent in such a situation are a source of anxiety. Freedom is scary. Some of the people at St. Michael's spoke about their fear—fear both of approaching change and of the possibility no change would occur.

But people looking at an unknown future do feel hopeful, as well as anxious. "I felt we could turn his leaving into a new beginning," said one member of Grace Church. Bishop Hillman wrote the people of St. Andrew's Church: "Whenever there is a vacancy in the ordained leadership of a congregation, that limb of the Body of Christ has a real opportunity to move, with excitement and joy, into new understandings of mission and ministry."

The moment of the minister's leaving is open in the sense that it is revealing, open in that it leads to an unknown future. It is also a moment open to outside intervention. The vacancy period is a natural time to look for consultative help. This help can be provided over a brief span of time, but it can have far-reaching consequences for the future of the congregation.

Vacancy Consultation: Goals and Methods

Bishop Shephard described his job as consultant to the calling committee at the Church of the Resurrection in these words: "What I'm doing now is to help you be clear about where this parish is and where you want to lead it." This way of speaking about the aims of vacancy consultation puts the primary emphasis on the parish's need to find out where it is going before it can start working on the secondary goal—to find the right kind of clergyman for the journey. The bishop's words make it clear that the people own the process and the parish. The ministry belongs to the congregation; only after that unique ministry has been determined will the congregation be able to decide what parts of it they will "hire out" and what kind of clergyman will best be able to perform those parts of the ministry.

Any parish undergoing a change in leadership lives through a process of several steps:

—terminating the relationship with the departing pastor

—planning the search process

—gathering information on such questions as: Who are we? What kind of leader do we need?

—writing a profile based on the data

—finding and screening names of candidates

—interviewing candidates

—choosing a candidate and issuing a call

—reaching an agreement with the chosen clergyman

—periodically reviewing the agreement and evaluating the work.

Some of these steps may receive more emphasis than others. Some may be followed in a carefully planned way, others almost unconsciously. But, in one way or another, the process is worked through. In some congregations, the consultant may be involved at every step; in others, he may help with only a few.

The stories of these fourteen churches show wide variety in the intensity and duration of the consultant's involvement in the congregation's vacancy process. In some cases, the consultant kept to the first task: assisting the congregation in deciding on their own direction. In other churches, the consultant was involved in subsequent steps, helping with the search and the negotiation of a contract between the congregation and the new minister. The wide variety in parishes, consultative styles, and the amount of consultative help available makes the broad spectrum of consultant involvement seem appropriate.

Perhaps advantages can be found in different degrees of involvement. One consultant who labored intensively over a long period of time was able to provide an interesting and useful series of training sessions on interviewing methods. On the other hand, there were signs that long and intensive consultations sometimes resulted in impatient clients. One parish fired the consultants at the point of reading the print-outs from the computer. "We can handle things now," the people said. There were also indications that when consultants helped parishes get started on a vacancy procedure and then left them to carry on independently, the parishes' sense of ownership of the process was enhanced. There were cases, however, in which consultants were not involved enough in the several steps of the process.

The stories seem to show a need for flexibility, not only in the intensity and duration of the consultation, but also in its style and design. The need for custom-built consultations was expressed by the group leaders who protested that "the design was too hard . . . we are a freewheeling discussion group parish and this is too organized." The parish that was in the process of deciding whether or not to call the associate indicated that different kinds of consultative procedures would have met their needs more adequately.

The Bishop

When the minister tells the congregation he is leaving, the members naturally turn first to their bishop. The initial encounter between representatives of the parish and the bishop has a crucial effect on the experience and outcome of the vacancy period. Consultant Martha Adams, after studying the data from several of these vacancy consultations, concluded:

The "common thread" in all these cases seems to be that the relationship of the congregation to the bishop certainly sets the tone for the beginning of the consultation. How he perceives them and how they perceive themselves—as in trouble or healthy; as moving toward growth or standing still; as resistant to self-examination or willing to enter it—may determine whether they enter the consultation with an air of hostility or excitement, and whether or not they see themselves as able to endure the frustrations which inevitably arise from a period of searching for direction and leadership.

Under ideal circumstances, the bishop is able to offer guidance, help and support to the parish during the vacancy period and represent the concerns of the larger community to the congregation as it considers its priorities, while at the same time allowing the parish to retain ownership of the process. However, problems may occur in the relationship between the bishop and the parish that make it impossible for him to make one or more of these offerings.

A letter from Bishop Falconer to the people of St. George's reveals the wish all bishops have to provide support, guidance, and help to the parish that has lost its minister. In his letter, the bishop shows his concern and interest, points out what he thinks is important about the vacancy period, and outlines his plans for being useful to the parish. Even though the story of Bishop Bunyan's diocese is a composite picture, he may well play all the helpful roles in one parish that he played in this story: confronter, group member ("just one of us"), provider of guidelines, consultant, pastor, stewardship trainer, supporter of the parish's autonomy, interpreter of the dynamics of the vacancy period, supply priest, personnel officer, manager of the diocesan system, leader of the evaluation session, and one who continually affirms new insights arrived at during the vacancy period.

If people are confused about where to turn when their clergyman announces his resignation, what they need most of all may be suggestions on how to proceed. One parishioner expressed the relief he felt after his bishop provided this kind of help. "I know it's going to be hard work, but now we know where to put in the work. None of us knew how you get a rector except maybe put an ad in the paper."

A parish in crisis may need to hear its bishop's plea ". . . that we not be disheartened—that this is a parish that will move into the future, scarred maybe, but into the future we will move and live and act." A bishop may provide help in a less direct way, by interpreting a congregation's history to a consultant. In some situations the most important supportive role the bishop needs to fill is that of pastor—to the clergyman who is leaving, to a divided congregation, or to a senior warden who is serving as "pastor" of the congregation. Guidance, help and support are provided in many different ways in different situations.

A second kind of offering the bishop often wishes to make is to represent wider, extraparochial and community concerns to the parish as it seeks to determine its mission. The bishop's role in representing "the big picture" to the parish seems particularly important, in view of the tendency in so many of these parishes to pull in, away from social concerns, and concentrate on taking care of themselves. There is a feeling of retrenchment, of poverty, of not having concern, time, or money for external demands. Many new clergymen are clearly told, "Your job is to stay home and take care of this parish."

If the bishop decides to press on such a parish his natural

concern for mission and ministry outside the parish walls, he may or may not be heard. Bishop Shephard's request that ecumenical and minority group concerns be added to the parish profile as "bishop's addenda" was received as helpful. So was the roasting he gave the committee one night for having become too ingrown. As one parishioner put it, "We had become so ingrown that we wouldn't even recognize the church in the next town. Some perspective!"

Bishop Falconer's efforts to get input from community leaders for the choice of a new rector for St. George's were accepted by the parish. But Bishop Hand's refusal to accept the parish profile until it expressed a concern for ministering to the minority group in the church's neighborhood was at least one cause of the vestry's decision to "buck the bishop." Many complex factors undoubtedly influence the willingness of a parish to listen to a bishop's broader concerns. The bishop's style of leadership, his use of power, and his willingness to let the parish own the process seem crucial.

A congregation who sees the bishop as a figure of paternal authority tends to react like a rebellious adolescent or, alternatively, a docile child. Rebellious people said things like "We felt as if our hands had been slapped," or "I resented that this job was taken away by the bishop, who didn't think we had enough sense to get our own [priest]."

If the congregation feels the bishop has imposed the consultant, they are likely to resist or reject the latter, or find him irrelevant. As the Diocese of Central New York handbook puts it, "the facilitator might as well pack up and go home if . . . the people in the parish feel he is a secret agent for the bishop." In one of our stories, an interviewer learned from the experience of a rebellious congregation that "parishes need opportunity to really 'buy in' and not use consultants as a 'must do' order from the bishop." If the consultant comes into the parish saying, "I am not the bishop's man," after he had clearly been *sent* by the bishop, a question arises whether he will be believed.

A parish whose character and history dispose it to respond compliantly to the bishop is likely to behave more like an obedient child. The people at St. David's heard their bishop saying that he would direct the process of providing a new rector. The reaction to the appearance of a consultant was, "Why do we have to go through this? All we want is a priest. Who's the bishop going to send us?" If the bishop is seen as the source of a new rector, there is little incentive to fool around with consultants. St. David's strongly resisted the suggestion that retrieval interviews be held to evaluate the consultant's work. And an opinion was expressed that the bishop, not the consultation, had produced the new rector—an opinion with which the interviewer agreed. One consultant who read this story pointed out that if a parish "plays the game" in order to get a new rector it is unlikely that the consultative process will have any lasting influence on the life style of the congregation.

The way people interpret a bishop's actions is influenced by many factors—by what the bishop intends to do, by a parish's characteristic style of reacting to persons in authority, also by the kinds of expectations parishioners and clergymen have of bishops. The whole problem is complicated by the fact that many bishops have been changing their styles of leadership and experimenting with more democratic methods, while people's expectations have not kept up with these changes. These lagging perceptions may cause people to see authoritarian behavior when it is not present, or to reject the bishop's efforts to let the parishes own the process, out of nostalgia for the "good old days." The clergyman who left St. Andrew's was impatient with the bishop's refusal to assign him to a mission in a unilateral kind of way. The parishioner who reacted to the vacancy process by saying, "The old way was better—the bishop knows the parish and the men," was not unique.

When consultation was seen as *imposed* by the bishop, the consultative process was regarded as *belonging to the bishop,* regardless of whether the parish responded like a biddable child or a freedom-fighter. But when the consultation was seen as *offered* by the bishop, it tended to be viewed, if accepted, as *belonging to the parish*—a tool they could use to help them accomplish a goal that was important to them. Some bishops who were concerned that the consultative process belongs to the parish made a point of offering the church its choice of several trained consultants.

The bishop who himself performs vacancy consultant services in his diocese has special problems in regard to his role image. Sunny Eberhart analyzed a consultation that Bishop Hillman had conducted in his diocese, and Eberhart reached this conclusion about the bishop's role as consultant: "I really don't think it works. It has nothing to do with the skills of the bishop or his awareness of people. It is just that the laymen in the parish do not see him as a consultant—they see him as the bishop. . . . John Hillman became aware of this after the [previous] consultation and added Jim Worth and Bill Eaglesman to the consultation at St. Andrew's." Besides adding other men to the team, Bishop Hillman made a point of withdrawing from the vacancy process after the initial stages so that the major part of the process was handled independently by the search committee and vestry. Retrieval interviews showed that they were conscious of being on their own and felt that they had directed the process that led to the selection of their new minister.

The special difficulties the bishop encounters in his role as consultant may be balanced by his special opportunities. He knows the past history of the parish, and he will play a part in its future. He can therefore, suggests Bishop John Wyatt, both provide ongoing support for the new life style that has been "tried on" during the consultation, and be held accountable for his work as consultant. He can do both these things by asking the vestry and new rector: "How can I improve what I am doing as consultant? I'm doing a lot of it and I need to learn."

Wyatt, bishop of Spokane and a helpful consultant to the author, has found that the first posthoneymoon disagreement between priest and people is a crucial moment:

If I take it as a reflection upon my skill or the adequacy of our procedure, I'm lost. If I simply move into a problem-solving stance, referring back to our experience during the search, and ahead toward the question, "What new resources do priest and people need to develop a more satisfying way of relating and working?" then I give powerful signals that this is not expected to be an *ideal* "marriage" but a growing relationship of real and imperfect human beings.

A chart of the degree of involvement of the bishops in these fourteen churches would be a broad spectrum, all the way from Bishop Webster, an interested, concerned onlooker, to Bishop Bunyan, with his "500 hats." The problem of role confusion is not limited to a Bishop Bunyan, with his multifaceted involvement in a parish's life. In a very different situation, a parishioner said suspiciously, "Bishops are human. They want to move certain people. I would not ask the bishop for names. He just wants certain ones to move and I didn't want any of them." This comment seems to express a fear that the bishop will recommend clergymen merely as a diocesan manager rather than out of concern for the parish.

Role confusion is, of course, compounded in a small diocese, where the bishop must perform many functions in the same parish. The bishop's clarity and openness about his own investment in the placement are essential. His carefulness in distinguishing his various functions can help him interpret the role changes to the people with whom he is working. Out of his struggles with the problems of role confusion, Bishop Wyatt says:

I believe it is extremely important for a bishop/consultant to surface the issue and express his own dilemma: "I want to be a consultant to aid you in your task. Obviously I am also the guy who will later have to put on his cope and mitre and make a decision as to whether or not he will approve calling the man you have decided upon. The only way I know of doing it is to ask you to help me monitor my behavior. If I seem to you to be getting in the way of your freedom, yell. I'm trying to learn how to be a more effective consultant, and I can't without your help."

If these problems—role confusion, the gap between episcopal styles and parish expectations, and most important, parish ownership of the vacancy process—can be adequately handled, the bishop is freed to make his special offerings as chief pastor to the parish in search of a minister.

The Funeral

The congregation's first reaction to the minister's departure is grief, the process of reacting to the experience of bereavement. Expressions of sorrow seem to be common, but not always unanimous at such times.

The wide variety of responses to a minister's departure in these fourteen cases may be grouped as follows:

Feelings of *grief, loss,* and *sadness* may find expression in despair, or they may lead parishioners to try to find a new minister just like the one they are losing. The consultants might well learn from these stories that parishioners need their feelings of grief treated with respect. They resent any behavior on the part of the consultant they feel is callous or oblivious of their bereavement. One member of the Church of the Holy Communion felt it was no time for "fun and games": "A parish which has been without a priest for some time doesn't feel like joking." A member of St. Barnabas's saw the rector's empty desk as a symbol of the congregation's loss and resented the consultant's putting his feet on the reverently guarded piece of furniture.

Anxiety, fear, and *panic* may appear as feelings that the parish will not survive, or as anger at delays in the process of obtaining a new rector. The handbook put out by the Diocese of Central New York for parishes in search of a rector says panic is a normal reaction: "Expect panic on all sides from nearly everyone that the congregation will dry up and blow away unless a new rector is found tomorrow." Richard J. Kirk, in "On the Calling and Care of Pastors," [1] points out that panic is an expression of strong dependence on the pastor. These stories seem to indicate that parishes do not panic with the loss of their clergyman when there is strong, independent lay leadership.

Guilt and *self-doubt* are frequent reactions of members. Feelings of guilt over past criticism of the pastor apparently lead to the attitude expressed in the maxim, "Speak no evil of the dead." One parishioner said, "I wondered why he was leaving; I wondered if we hadn't done something he wanted us to do," sounding like a bereaved child who feels he is being deserted because of his own insufficiency.

Anger at the rector is also mentioned as an incidental response in a couple of other parishes. Such anger was expressed most strongly by a parish that accepted its rector's resignation after a hostile confrontation. It may well occur more often than it is reported. Since these stories focus on the period following the departure of the rector, data on feelings of anger directed toward him are probably minimized. In two of the three churches that asked for the rector's resignation, however, anger between the pro- and anti-firing parties led to polarization of the parish. The senior warden at St. Andrew's, who tried to embrace both sides of the division, was agonizingly torn by the situation, and described himself as feeling "crushed, decapitated." The third church that asked for and received the rector's resignation also experienced division, and the vestry nervously anticipated attack by other parishioners.

Understanding and self-confidence, along with expressions of grief, characterized the response of St. Barnabas's parishioners to the loss of their rector. This indicates that when the lay leadership is strong, the parish is able to make an adult-to-adult response, and even to say, "We were glad for his opportunity." This adult response stands out in strong contrast to the "bereaved child" reaction found in more dependent parishes. Bishop Wyatt points out that there is a relationship between the way a congregation sees its rector and its ability to let him go. If the congregation has really loved its rector in the sense of seeing him realistically as a human being, rather than as an idealized role figure, and being aware of his real functions in the parish, the people will be able to let one clergyman go and welcome another. An open style on the part of the rector makes this kind of love possible.

Feelings of relief or a lack of strong reactions were reported in some parishes. A response lacking in strong feeling seemed natural in churches where the pastorate had not been firmly established, because of its temporary character, because of illness or frequent absence on the part of the minister, or because the clergyman's predecessor had not been laid to rest.

Again and again, the stories reveal how important it is for a congregation to be aware of, express, and deal with its own peculiar constellation of grief reactions before it is ready to embrace a new pastoral relationship. (In order to help parishes do this, Loren Mead has suggested that the standing liturgical commission provide a service for the termination of a pastorate.) In one case, the continuing visits of the former minister held up the process of terminating one ministry and beginning another. In a couple of cases, the failure to work through the grief process resulted in pastorates that could not be established, or that were remembered as practically nonexistent. Parishes that fail to deal with destructive patterns often are parishes that repeatedly fire their pastors.

John Fletcher, director of Inter/Met, has called loss and pain "a garden, from which good things can grow." An acceptance of the loss of a clergyman makes possible the open moment of the vacancy period. "I was sorry to see him go, but also I felt we could turn his leaving into a new beginning," said a member of Grace Church.

Whatever grief reactions a congregation experiences when it loses its pastor, an essential part of the consultant's job is to help the parish work through its feelings about this loss. In many of the stories, working out the feelings of loss, guilt, and anger was a central task. In some cases it was not possible to resolve these feelings during the period of the consultation. In one such parish, people still felt that an important offering by the consultants had been to help them talk openly about the former rector for the first time. To surface these feelings makes it possible to work through them in the future. St. Barnabas's new rector saw an advantage in the length of the consultation period in that it gave members "time to grieve."

In most of these parishes the consultant helped the congregation become aware of and deal with feelings of loss after the rector had left the parish. A letter from the Rev. Kenneth J. Allen, training and education officer for the Diocese of

Los Angeles, to Loren B. Mead suggests an additional way of working with these feelings: "It seems to me that there is a place for thinking about how closure might be worked on while the priest and congregation are still in relationship. . . . A guy may be aware of taking care of the administrative aspects of closure, but I doubt that we have paid sufficient attention to the emotional aspects." The Rev. James R. Adams, reflecting on his departure from two parishes, also concludes that members were much better able to deal with his leaving when he spent time talking with them about it than when he did not.

Many of these stories indicate that a consultant often needs to broaden his concept of grief work. The feelings of loss, anxiety, guilt, and anger may be reactions, not only to the departure of one person, but to a whole series of painful events in the congregation's history—events that need to be looked at honestly and understood before the congregation can move on with a stance of openness to new experiences. In one church, the consultant included games in his design that "forced people to speak to each other who had not spoken in thirty years." In more than one parish, the process of "opening old wounds" was seen as a significant part of the consultation.

The Calling Committee

On being faced with the loss of its clergyman, one of the congregation's first tasks is to form a calling or search committee. A number of the fourteen parishes learned some things from their experiences with the composition, communication problems, and general effectiveness of calling committees. The two parishes in which the consultant worked with a "pick-up group," rather than a formally constituted calling or search committee, found that it didn't work. A task force composed of "whoever showed up" lacked the necessary authority and decision-making power. At the other end of the spectrum, calling committees created by the unilateral action of the former rector or senior warden ran into trouble. The former rector's selection of a number of calling committee members was seen as his effort to control the selection of his successor. The senior warden who had become anxious about the leadership vacuum and had announced the calling committee at the same time the rector announced his departure aroused the anger of other parishioners.

In some cases the calling committee was identical with the vestry. One church found problems with this practice in that old vestry conflicts were carried into the calling committee, hindering its work, and other people who needed to have a voice in the proceedings were not present. One consultant felt that "the committee should have vestry linkages, but not be a totally controlled committee. Once they make a decision, it should be their responsibility to sell the man to the vestry." William E. Swing's experience as a vacancy consultant led him to conclude that lack of sufficient vestry representation on a calling committee can result in low vestry involvement in the committee's work. Guidelines for vacancy procedures in the Diocese of Spokane make clear that the bishop/consultant's contract is with the vestry or bishop's committee, whom the bishop serves by working with the search committee. The search committee shares a tentative profile with the vestry, which revises the profile, returning it to the committee as a charge for that group's subsequent work.

Parishes that made a special effort to see that many groups and factions in the parish, including people who were "on the outs" or irregular in church attendance, were represented on the committee seemed to feel that this had been a useful decision. One possible result of the openness of the vacancy experience is that new groups will exert influence in the congregation's life. A parish that had chosen a large and representative calling committee concluded that this had helped more people feel they had an "ego investment" in the decision, and that "a larger team picks a man and will support him." In these churches, people felt that their ownership of the parish and the decision process had been enhanced.

Ownership was also heightened when efforts were made to involve a large number of members in gathering data and setting priorities, and when the committee worked to keep the congregation informed of its progress. In one parish in which a selected group of members was invited to work with the consultant there were feelings that the invitation should have been open. Efforts to increase the number of parishioners involved later on in the process did not prove very successful. In another church, the committee's refusal to involve a wider group of members was at least one factor in the committee's being distrusted by the congregation. The retrieval team concluded that "consultants must concentrate from the beginning on helping their clients to seek input from the total system, and to report out often and in many forms." Kirk adds, "Frequent communication about the steps being taken can reduce some of the panic generated by the absence of a 'regular' pastor." [2]

Working with Data and Priorities

The bishop's help having been sought, the calling committee appointed, and the consultant selected, the next major task is to get input from the congregation. The churches used several methods of gathering data—of finding out from as many people as possible what was important to them about the church, what they felt the problems were, where they thought the parish ought to be heading, and what kind of leadership qualities and styles they wanted in a new rector. Questionnaires tended to produce a low rate of return and a low level of involvement, but they did yield helpful data. The use of interviews had the advantage of allowing the parish to press for responses from the disaffected. Parish meetings resulted in a high level of involvement, with people getting very angry in a few cases, and more often feeling that the experience had been a positive and important one. The process was often seen as more important than the data. As one interviewee exclaimed, "What I thought was important was the doing, the action, the process—that's what was important. The report could have been thrown in the trash can." A supplementary method of data gathering was used by the bishop who met with community leaders to get their input. This experiment seemed to be promising. Community representatives accepted the opportunity enthusiastically; their input differed from that of the parish, but was taken into account by the search committee and may well have helped to increase its sense of responsibility to the world outside the church doors.

The stories indicate that the information gathered was used more enthusiastically by the prospective rector than by the members. The calling committee used the data to write the profile. After this the information, one assumes from the lack of any further reference, met up with that trash can mentioned earlier. The candidates, however, are generally deeply impressed by the data, and feel they have been given a clear and honest picture of the parish. (The context of the candidates' comments about "data" often indicates that they were talking about the report or profile that was written on the basis of the data.)

Following the gathering of data, the calling committee sifts through this mass of input to determine priorities and to write a profile of the parish and the leadership needed. The congregation, as it draws up its leadership profile, often seems to have all the romantic character of a young man or woman dreaming about the person he or she will marry. People become aware of the exaggerated quality of these dreams, and make wry or humorous comments:

Even Jesus Christ wouldn't meet our specifications. . . .

We drew up a profile just a slight bit below [the new rector]—if the water was a little muddy he could walk on it. In some ways it was too idealistic. We knew it was too much.

Of course, we wanted a saint to fall out of the sky—guess he would have been lonesome.

We wanted a thirty-year-old ex-Confederate general.

Data gathering, priority setting, and profile writing are often recalled as extremely important and helpful stages of the consultation. Members feel that they have taken a good look at themselves, become clear about their priorities, and resolved some important issues in the church's life. "The information helped us get a man; the material was used," said one parishioner. Many of the stories reveal a clear correlation between the priorities and the kind of candidate selected. Candidates receive useful information from the profiles and are often attracted by their honesty:

There were some major factors that impressed me to come here— their willingness to admit difficulties, frankly. They did not bring me here under false pretenses. . . .

It was quite different from my past experience of the soft sell at the time of calling. It was helpful to me to look at both strengths and weaknesses.

Several consultants feel that the profile's usefulness ought not to be ended by the calling of a new man. Bishop Wyatt uses the profile in his meeting with new priest and vestry "to hold parish leaders responsible for what they said, to have the freedom to restate it and to find in the process a model for dealing with imperfect behavior." Though it is constantly subject to revision, the profile needs to remain an important piece of lore for the congregation. If the new clarity about the congregation's strengths, problems, and goals is never referred to or supported after a new clergyman has been found, it cannot be sustained.

Finding a New Minister

Between the writing of the profile and the negotiation of the contract with the new clergyman, the consultants in our stories were typically not involved in the parishes. One consultant had the job of assisting the calling committee in interviewing potential candidates and helped them avoid an unsuitable "marriage." But, in general, participants seemed to feel that this was a time for the parish to make a decision on its own. In some cases the consultant was eased out of the process or definitely fired at this stage. It would appear that in several of these cases the contract between the consultant and the congregation did not clearly state the steps in the vacancy process in which the consultant would be involved.

Following the profile-writing stage, with its dreams of grandeur, comes what Bishop Wyatt calls "an awkwardness stage. It seems that the first question in facing an actual priest who might come is 'Will he like us? Will he want to come? Dare we ask? He might say no.' " Bishop Hillman also saw an "inferiority sense" in parishes at this point in the proceedings. The diffidence of people at Otter Gap and Hatchery Dam was evident when they said, "We . . . couldn't expect to get someone like the bishop."

At this point in the selection process there are a number of references to the CDO, New York, or the computer. These are different ways of speaking about the computerized personnel files in the Clergy Deployment Office in New York, through which Episcopal parishes secure names of possible candidates. One is struck by the number of times negative comments are made about "the great computer back East." A rector says with pride, "*I* didn't come out of the computer." Others indicate confusion about the forms and the print-outs, or impatience with the time this process takes.

It is interesting that the parishes use this tool universally, and that almost all of them find it helpful, and yet the negative comments are there. It may be that there is an aversion to using a machine in a process that in every case seems warmly human. It may feel like blasphemy to try to replace dearly beloved Father X by filling in blanks on a form. Certainly people seem to have a problem with their feelings at this point. Part of the problem may also be that people have unreal expectations of the computer, which can be useful at only one point in a complex task.

The comments suggest that these feelings need to be taken seriously by consultants or bishops who help the committees work with the forms and print-outs. Both the usefulness of the computer as a tool giving access to information and the human dimension of the interviewing and decision-making need to be affirmed. Care must be taken not to raise unreal expectations. It would probably be wise, also, to take seriously the difficulties calling committees find with the process, arranging careful training and orientation for those who work with the calling committee at this point.

One further learning that seems to emerge from the calling stage is that the prospective rector needs to learn something about the community as well as about the church. Often the profiles are helpful in providing an analysis of the community. The senior warden at the Church of the Resurrection was impressed with the way Father LeJeune, during his visit, took the opportunity to go to businesses in town and talk with people and to look at the community to get an overall picture. With no previous awareness of Live Oak's life style, the new rector of St. David's found himself facing problems for which he hadn't bargained.

Finally the long and hard work to terminate the previous pastorate, gather data, write a profile, find candidates' names, and interview prospective clergymen comes to an end. A call is extended and accepted. The void in the congregation's life that had brought grief, anxiety, guilt, or anger has been closed. By the time a new minister has been found, retrieval interviews in these fourteen churches indicate that good—or even marvelous—things have grown out of the experience of losing the previous pastor. When the new minister arrives on the scene, people tend to feel that all their hopes have been fulfilled. With the exception of the parish that had not completed the process of deciding whether to call the associate, the evaluation of the new rector was very positive in all these churches. In a parish concerned about involving young people, the new rector invited sixty young members to his house. Two parishioners reported the number as two hundred. Marriage metaphors like "falling in love" and "honeymoon" are frequently used in describing the relationship between the new clergyman and his congregation. Bishop Hillman, in his letter to the people of St. Andrew's, reminded them of the pertinence of the words of the marriage ritual to the choice of a new rector.

In many of the parishes, the joy of this honeymoon period clearly indicates that the vacancy process has resulted in a good match. But the parish's transformation from bereaved child to lover has other rich and complex human dimensions. The lost father has been mourned. The new relationship is described as a "marriage." Kirk pointed out that the new clergyman is sometimes seen as a member of a new generation. The fact that the new rector is there because he was chosen by the congregation is fresh in everyone's mind: "We chose him; he accepted us; he's ours; he's wonderful." (The former rector was also chosen by the congregation, but the memory of this choice has grown dim.) There hasn't been time to become dependent on the new minister, or to discover his rough edges. Bishop Wyatt describes the honeymoon period in this way: "After acceptance of the call, the priest comes with some eagerness. The laity are aware that he does not yet know all the skeletons. Those whose dependencies upon the previous priest were unresolved try the new man out for size. . . ."

The honeymoon character of the new relationship reflects, in part, the human tendency to overvalue a new object—a sweetheart, a new baby, a new job, or a new rector. As the new object is gazed upon uncritically, the visual field is contracted. As the popular song puts it, "I only have eyes for you," and there is temporary loss of perspective.

In some cases, the congregation's delighted feelings during the honeymoon period may also reflect relief at the end of an anxious time. In other churches, lay people may be expressing the heightened sense of ownership and strengthened leadership ability that have resulted from functioning successfully without a professional leader for a time. As the honeymoon period wears off, it will be important to bring to the relationship the soberness, honesty, discipline, and mutual responsibility that any good marriage requires. Bishop Shephard's pre-Christmas meeting with the new vestry of the Church of the Resurrection is an example of the kind of support that could bring a post-honeymoon candor to the relationship. The profile that had been written six months earlier probably contained some seductive language, some "chamber of commerce blurbs," aimed at attracting a new rector. Now the profile can be viewed from a new perspective and revised where necessary. Priest and vestry can rethink their goals, their plans for carrying them out and evaluating them. The problem-solving stance thus established is not unlike that of a husband and wife taking a course in parent effectiveness training prior to the birth of their first child.

Structures for Accountability—Contracts and Evaluation

"Accountability" is a word that sums up a final theme appearing, not only in Bishop Shephard's work with the Church of the Resurrection, but throughout the stories. In almost every case, some method is used to try to establish clarity between the people and their new minister about how he can function effectively in the areas the congregation has identified as its unique mission. The structures chosen most often to help parishes and clergymen be accountable are contracts and evaluation. Both are processes for helping the congregation and its minister focus on their joint priorities.

Bishop Shephard met with the vestry and new rector of the Church of the Resurrection to help them rethink the priorities together. The bishop reported: "We identified six areas in which both priest and people were in substantial agreement. The vestry at that point took kindly to my suggestion that the rector, before the next vestry meeting, write out a proposal of what he would like to accomplish on those six in the next twelve months and work out an agreement with them to accomplish those things. . . . At the end of twelve months, they plan to meet for an accountability session to see how well they've done."

The profile is a basic document at this stage. William E. Swing found it important in determining the character of his first year in a new parish. Because the congregation has worked to become clear about its task, and has chosen a clergyman whose leadership qualities are appropriate for that ministry, the new rector has a clear sense of direction for his ministry. "I had a mandate," says Swing. "I knew what they wanted me to do. I went ahead and made bold changes, and the congregation was right behind me."

Two of the stories show in a particularly dramatic way how important it is for a congregation and its pastor to have structures that help them to keep the priorities in sight, adjusting them when necessary; to evaluate efforts in the light of goals; and to hold one another accountable for the responsibilities undertaken. One is the story of St. Mary's, where, in the absence of a contract or any stated priorities, the new rector was "breaking his neck to do everything." The other is the story of St. Andrew's, a striking example of how a congregation's history can push members toward realizing their need to hold the rector accountable. It was even suggested that a rector be hired on a year-to-year basis, and traces of this suggestion turned up in the contract and evaluation procedures eventually adopted.

These stories also illustrate how many times the need for accountability structures is misunderstood, and how often the idea of a contract meets with resistance. In one parish in which the drawing up of a contract was resisted as a sign of distrust, a member protested that their rector was "an honest and respectable clergyman!" When the contract was negotiated, however, these same people experienced a heightened sense of inclusion in the work. Another response to the idea of contracts or evaluation appeared in the two parishes with charismatic groups. These groups tended to distrust the procedures involved in accountability, feeling that they might indicate lack of confidence in the power of God to keep the relationship clear between minister and people. These stories suggest, however, that the relationship can become confused and unproductive, no matter how devoted the pastor and people.

Consultants helped parishes negotiate contracts and make plans for periodic evaluation in a number of ways. One consultant had the vestry compare their job description for their new rector with the man's position paper and helped them work with the similarities and differences. Another consultant worked with sixty parishioners over a weekend to find out what they wanted their clergyman to be doing. They were excited about the process, the openness, the new understanding of how their rector spent his time. This consultant thought that it had been an advantage to postpone the negotiation of a contract until the new minister had been in the parish for a few weeks.

Bishop Bunyan planned to ask for feedback on his consultation "first of all, to legitimatize evaluation. . . . The second question has to do with, given your expectations as parish leaders, how has this particular priest been meeting them? The other question is to the priest—given your understanding of these congregations before you came, what has surprised you?"

The process through which the bishop had helped the congregation move in its search for a new rector was not completed now that a new man had been found, but was, rather, an experiment with a more satisfying way of living and working. Knowing that new life styles are hard to maintain, the bishop would continue to use his visits to the parish as opportunities to support them. In more than one parish, the visits of the PTP retrieval team dramatized the need of the consulted church for ongoing support. Both the Littlehouse/Lovington team and Sunny Eberhart were able to see trouble brewing and flash an SOS to the bishop. Bishop Hillman felt that Eberhart's warning about communication problems between a new clergyman and a church (whose story is not included here) had been worth the total cost of retrieval interviews in his diocese.

Contracts and evaluations, then, are the most common structures developed to help the congregation and minister be accountable to each other. This holds true whether or not the contract or evaluation system was ever written down. Most of these parishes did not have written documents describing the contract or evaluation procedure. It is, however, important to try to clarify expectations so that they will be open and aboveboard rather than under the table. One has a feeling that in a number of cases the consultants helped the minister and the congregation *start* a process by which they could continue to talk to each other about how the work of ministry was going on. To the extent that this proves to be true, the congregation and the minister will be better equipped to continue reevaluating their work together, adjusting to new priorities as they arise, phasing out things that cease to be important—all in a normal process of mutual accountability rather than an atmosphere of acute conflict or confrontation. To the extent that this happens, the congregations will have developed their own structures of accountability, whether or not they ever write a contract or hold a formal evaluation.

Evaluating the Vacancy Consultations

In "On the Calling and Care of Pastors," Richard J. Kirk describes the plight of unhappy clergymen "who feel that their talents are not being utilized or appreciated" and parishioners who are "unhappy with the performance of their pastor because in some way he fails to meet their expectations of him." [3] One way of evaluating vacancy consultations is to try to determine whether they tend to produce relationships in which clergy and people are *not* unhappy with each other, whether they help to put "the right man in the right place at the right time," whether, to put it briefly, they "work." Another, more open-ended kind of evaluation would seek to analyze the general effects of the vacancy consultation upon the congregation's ongoing life.

There are some difficulties in the task of deciding, on the basis of these fourteen churches' experiences, whether vacancy consultation works. The fact that retrieval interviews were carried on during the honeymoon period makes it difficult to distinguish two reactions. One is the positive response based on a conviction that clear priorities led to the choice of this clergyman; the other is enthusiasm springing primarily from the overvaluation of a new object. A second set of retrieval interviews, held after the rector and parish had lived together for a year, would be helpful in clarifying these reactions and would also give indications of the degree to which life-style changes were maintained.

There are additional difficulties in that, for a variety of reasons, some of the consultations were unable to fulfill their intended purpose. Two churches rejected the vacancy consultation in rejecting the bishop's power; one allowed the consultation, but did not regard it as relevant to the process of obtaining a new rector; one found the consultation did not speak to the dynamics of the parish situation; and in a couple of cases the consultative process did not appear to be germane because the rector was regarded as "sent" rather than "chosen." In most of these churches the vacancy consultation was seen as helpful in various important ways—for example, in facilitating self-examination, openness, more satisfying interpersonal relations, personal growth. Important learnings can be drawn from all these cases. Consultants studying the files of these churches can learn how to conduct more effective vacancy consultations.

An additional complication for evaluation is illustrated most clearly in the stories of St. Michael's and St. Paul's. The choice of a rector can never be made on purely logical grounds, but is at least partly, and in some cases primarily, dependent on the chemistry between the clergyman and the parish. "I just liked him," said one committee member in explaining his choice of Mark Newman. Others said, "We like Mark, but if we compared Mark's profile and our profile they wouldn't have jibed." A parishioner at St. Paul's made the same point: "The purpose of the profile was to bring some objectivity into the whole thing. But the selection was still made on a subjective basis. . . . . Do you like the guy?" Obviously no attempt should be made to encourage people to abandon the human, intuitive grounds for their decisions, but the presence, and the power, of such grounds enriches and complicates the analysis of vacancy consultations. It also underlines the importance of postcalling procedures that help parish and priest to base their relationship in reality.

One further factor needs to be taken into account in evaluating the success of the consultations. Again and again in the stories there appear comments from vestries, parishioners, and clergymen that vacancy consultations are new, strange, and therefore, for some people, to be resisted. It is hard to imagine a person talking about "this new thing the bishop wants us to do" in tones of approval or enthusiasm. Long-held expectations about how a new minister comes to a church were being countered, and this experience was seldom easy. Bishop Falconer looked forward to a time when all the experimenting would produce commonly accepted procedures. Further trial and error and further research will be needed to establish the most effective ways to help parishes work through the vacancy experience. At the time these consultations were held, however, some resistance to experiments needs to be taken into account as a factor in the evaluation.

After all these complications and difficulties have been assessed, however, it is evident that in at least half these parishes there was a significant correlation between the church's perception of its priorities and problems and the choice of a new minister. The people of Grace Church, for example, wanted a conservative clergyman who would involve more young people in the parish, yet the consultation helped them arrive at some perception of a "lack of consistency" in their goals. The new rector concluded, ". . . we both wanted much the same things, with one exception—their data called for no change." One member reflected, "Rufus just seemed to fit. He is a fairly conservative, energetic young family man." Another challenged, "I'll bet you conservatives that you will be changing more with this man than with a liberal."

Parishioners of St. John's felt that their painful history required the "strong, sure, loving, spiritual leadership" of a pastor who could build bridges between divided segments of the parish. Both people and new rector were clear that this kind of pastoral care was the first priority in the decision to call Heartfield and in the ongoing life of the parish. It seems clear that the people of the Church of the Resurrection wanted, and got, a priest who promised to help them appeal to young families and to counter ingrown tendencies.

In two other cases, the *process* of the consultation seemed to contribute to the correlation between the priorities and the choice of a new parson. At St. Andrew's, people were tremendously concerned about healing the rift caused by firing the former rector. The methods by which the new rector was chosen helped to increase the congregation's ability to unite behind the new minister; a large and representative calling committee worked together and made efforts to communicate with the rest of the parish. Members of St. George's felt that apathy and lack of enthusiasm constituted the parish's chief problem. The bishop's decision to consult with local leaders about the qualities needed in a new rector seems to have been made, in part, to challenge that apathy. An interviewee felt that the bishop and consultants "carried the prod." The new rector, who was described as a "fireball," and had the people "working like dogs," seemed an appropriate choice.

Apart from his or her usefulness in helping a parish decide on and find the kind of leadership it needs, the consultant can help the community experience some new, useful ways of living and working. Part of the openness of the vacancy period results from the fact that, with the departure of the previous rector, old patterns have been loosened up. New hopes emerge, and in order to realize these hopes people are often willing to experiment with new understandings, attitudes, and ways of working together. As consultant Rogers put it, his job was "life-style intervention."

Many different kinds of new understandings and attitudes appear as a result of the consultants' work with the congregations: an understanding that loss is a part of life, and that feelings about that loss need to be faced and dealt with; a new realization of the power of the congregation's history; new clarity about the parish's problems and priorities; a new realism about the clergyman's job; renewed self-confidence and hope for the future.

Communities experiment with new norms; involving the whole congregation in decision-making; opening communication—among individual parishioners and subgroups, between people and pastor, and between parish and bishop; determining goals and setting priorities; being willing to open up conflict situations and find new ways of handling them; developing clear and open mutual expectations between clergyman and people; conducting periodic evaluations; and being open to the idea of asking for and receiving help when it is needed. Obviously not all, or even most, of these new understandings and norms appear in every case. The question must also be raised to what extent the changes will become a lasting part of the congregation's way of life—a question that will need to be answered by further research.

In many cases, the consultant's work enhanced some of the positive effects of the vacancy period. Parish after parish had the experience that, in the absence of an official leader, the indigenous leadership of the parish was free to emerge. The people could experience their own strength. Lay people reported that the experience of the vacancy was one of ownership ("We realized that it was *our* ministry"), pride ("We did it!"), involvement ("Everybody pitched in"), commitment ("We would have gone out and fought dragons for St. Michael's!"), and joy ("We've been shown what we *can* do and we like it.")

The consultant can help the people appropriate these benefits of the vacancy period. It is clearly not his parish—he comes into the situation from outside, with no immediate stake, claims, or power in the parish. He is trained to discourage people's attempts to become dependent on him: Royall Rogers, at St. Luke's Church, refused to do the parishioners' work for them; Bishop Hillman could "bite his tongue" and resist the temptation to suggest candidates prematurely. If his clients later wonder whether his services were necessary, he can entertain the possibility that his efforts were successful.

The Rev. Ed White, reflecting on some of these stories, says:

The consultant is an artist, not a technician. He makes a heavy personal investment in the process and in the people. He is there more to improve the quality of common life of the decision makers than to influence the decisions. He models behaviors that become contagious. He helps the local leadership to discover the richness within themselves. When he is finished the people are sorry to see him go, they are grateful, but they are less dependent upon him than when he came.

The consultant can work toward the empowerment of the local church, as did Bishop Bunyan, when he helped members to feel that "it was all right for them to use their power." The consultant can help members to find "a way of accepting responsibility," and he, or the bishop, can help them maintain this new level of responsibility in their relationship with a new minister. In helping members to own the decision to call a new rector, the consultant can help them arrive at a heightened sense of ownership of their parish. The open moment of the vacancy period can provide opportunities for people to say with new conviction, "This is our church."

Notes

Preface

1. Sensing that the reference to a congregation without a pastor as a "vacant congregation" was symptomatic of a clergy-oriented mentality, the attempt was made to rename the project "Parish Consultation in Clergy Placement," but Vacancy Consultation it was, and Vacancy Consultation it has remained.

2. In one diocese with which a contract was developed, *no* vacancies occurred during the test period. The active data, therefore, come from nine dioceses.

3. The dioceses were selected at least partially because they had access to persons of known consulting experience.

Introduction

1. Inter/Met stands for Interfaith Metropolitan Theological Education, Inc., a creative experiment in seminary training that is located in Washington, D.C.

2. The Clergy Deployment Office is maintained at the headquarters of the Episcopal Church in New York City. It assists congregations in locating clergy. A major resource is a system of personnel profiles available by computer print-out. Many stories in this book refer to "the computer," "CDO," "The Clergy Office," or "The Deployment Office." All are references to this agency and its work. Other denominations have similar offices with similar functions.

St. Luke's Church

1. The "charismatic movement" refers to a movement within the churches of a group of people particularly responsive to and moved by the Holy Spirit. In this book no attempt is made to deal with the substantive issues of that movement. It is described here simply as the way one (sometimes large, sometimes small) subgroup within a parish sees itself and how it functions in relation to other subgroups.

Reflections on the Case Histories

1. Richard J. Kirk, "On the Calling and Care of Pastors," ch. 2 in *Patterns in Parish Development,* ed. by Celia A. Hahn (New York: Seabury Press, 1974).
2. Ibid.
3. Ibid.